William Saumarez Smith

Obstacles to Missionary Success Among the Heathen

An Essay, Which Obtained the Maitland Prize for the Year 1867

William Saumarez Smith

Obstacles to Missionary Success Among the Heathen
An Essay, Which Obtained the Maitland Prize for the Year 1867

ISBN/EAN: 9783743395206

Manufactured in Europe, USA, Canada, Australia, Japa

Cover: Foto ©Thomas Meinert / pixelio.de

Manufactured and distributed by brebook publishing software (www.brebook.com)

William Saumarez Smith

Obstacles to Missionary Success Among the Heathen

CONTENTS.

CHAPTER I.
INTRODUCTORY . . . . 1 (PAGE)

CHAPTER II.
OBSTACLES TO MISSIONARY SUCCESS . . 10

CHAPTER III.
RECAPITULATION, AND CONCLUDING REMARKS . . 97

APPENDIX 111

Ὑμεῖς ἐστε τὸ ἅλας τῆς γῆς· ἐὰν δὲ τὸ ἅλας μωρανθῇ ἐν τίνι ἁλισθήσεται;

"When the truth and power of religion is separated from the profession thereof, a man's religion is nothing worth; for in this case there is a small difference 'twixt an Israelite and an Ishmaelite; 'twixt a circumcised Hebrew and an uncircumcised Philistine; 'twixt a baptized Englishman and an unwashen Turk: For the barren fig tree in God's orchard is in no better case than the bramble in the wilderness; for God will lap them both up in the same bundle of condemnation; it being all one to deny the faith, and not soundly and sincerely to profess it."

TERRY (*Voyage to East India.* 1655).

CHAPTER I.

INTRODUCTORY.

The History of the Christian Church is, pre-eminently, a history of Christian missions. In the present condition of high civilization, and in an age which has seen marvellous developments of scientific knowledge in its application to the necessities and interests of the human race, we are apt to lose sight of this important fact. Christianity has been so long established as an integral part of our social system that it requires some effort of thought to conceive of our ancestors in Britain, as naked savages, painted with woad, their towns "mere clusters of huts," and their religion a dark and cruel superstition, whilst the greater part of Europe was a jungle of wild forest, overrun by barbarous tribes, who must have been viewed by the Romans much in the same light as the cannibals of New Zealand, or the natives of Tahiti, were looked upon by the Europeans who first had intercourse with them.

Mighty indeed is the change which has been produced by that intricate process which we call civilization. The elements of this process, or complex fact, have been various. But there can be no question that the most powerful cause of the intellectual, social, and moral elevation of Europe above the other nations of the world was the spread of the Christian religion. And this was effected, under the overruling Providence of God, by the agency of *missionaries,*—"apostles," sent ones,—who, "beginning at Jerusalem[1]," preached repentance and remission of sins, in the name of Christ, among all nations. Nor can we think of what Europe owes to such men as Patrick, and Columba, and Ulphilas, and Severinus, without feeling that the indifference with which missionary efforts have been often viewed by men of politics, of science, and of literature, in modern times, is as unphilosophical in respect of what is to be learnt from history as it is unfaithful in respect of what is claimed by religion.

But our present subject belongs neither to the Apostolic nor to the Mediæval period of Church History. The sad fact of which it speaks,—namely, the hindrance to missionary success arising from the unchristian conduct of professed Christians,—might indeed be illustrated from both periods. The records of the New Testament, and the chronicles of ecclesiastical history in the 'dark ages,' alike bear witness to that development of worldly and carnal principles "in frail and erring human nature" which runs parallel with the development of Christianity itself[2], and continually places error by the side of, and blended with, truth;— a development, too, which, even where the form of sound doctrine may be preserved, is often dismally

---

[1] Luke xxiv. 47.
[2] See A. Butler's *Letters on Romanism,* L. II.

displayed in laxity of moral self-restraint, and looseness of living. The "perilous times" of which the Apostle Paul speaks in one of his letters to the youthful Bishop of Ephesus[1], when men should have a form of godliness while they denied the power thereof, have lasted since the Apostle's day down to our own times; and although, before the time of Constantine, the circumstances of the case did not allow of any extensive manifestation of corruption in the Christian community, ever since the Christian religion became the dominant and generally recognized creed we can trace the operation of corruption going on side by side with that of expansion and growth. The subject, however, with which we are at present concerned, evidently belongs to the later period of modern history, in which Europe is regarded as the source of Christian civilization. We are invited to treat of

The obstacles to missionary success among the heathen which have resulted from the defective moral and religious condition of Europeans, settlers, and others with whom they have associated.

This method of stating the subject pre-supposes the fact that Europe is professedly Christian, and has recognized the duty of sending Christian missionaries to the heathen; and it implies the extension of international intercourse consequent upon the increased facilities of navigation and commerce which date from the end of the fifteenth century.

The best commencement, therefore, of the essay will

---

[1] 2 Tim. iii. 1—5.

be a brief historical sketch of missionary enterprise since the Reformation. This must be followed by an attempt to bring under some sort of classification the obstacles which have been put in the way of missionary success by the irreligious conduct of nominal Christians. And the essay may be fitly concluded by a few remarks upon the intimate connexion between Christianity and Civilization, and the interdependence of missionary success abroad and evangelization at home.

The sixteenth century presents no annals of Protestant missions, unless we consider as such the feeble attempts made by a small body of French and Swiss Protestants[1] in Brazil, or the endeavour of Gustavus Vasa to introduce Christianity among the neglected Laplanders. But it is the most famous century for Roman Catholic missions. The maritime expeditions of the Portuguese and Spaniards were, from the first, inseparably connected with missionary efforts; and in all the early voyages for conquest or for commerce we trace a distinct religious motive mixed with political and mercantile schemes. How far that motive prevailed, and to what extent it was sincere, may be questioned, but that it did exist there cannot be a doubt. Indeed, from the time of the famous Papal grant to the Portuguese Crown in 1441[2], the object most prominently

---

[1] The colony was founded as an asylum for persecuted Huguenots; and the missionary efforts were but few, and only a secondary object. The disastrous termination of the colony and mission was due to the treachery of Villegagnon, who had first proposed the plan to Admiral Coligny. See Brown's *History of the Propagation of Christianity*, Ch. I.

[2] "The sovereign pontiff made a perpetual donation to the crown of

put forward as the incentive to further discoveries was the spread of the Catholic faith; and whatever may have been the mixed motives of the adventurers who joined the expeditions, some of the chief promoters of these expeditions,—such as Prince Henry of Portugal, and Queen Isabella of Spain,—were doubtless actuated by a sincere desire to extend the knowledge of the Christian religion, and the influence of the Christian Church.

So early as 1484 we find mention of an African chief sending an embassy to the King of Portugal, and requesting him to send priests to his dominions. The result of this embassy was the Portuguese mission to Congo, which attained considerable success[1]. The Spanish conquests in America, and the Portuguese acquisitions, both in South America and in India, gave a large scope to missionary enterprise: and the various monastic orders, especially the new 'Society of Jesus,' furnished an abundant supply of agents. In 1542 Xavier landed at Goa. In 1549 a Jesuit mission was sent to Brazil by King John III. of Portugal. In 1583 Ricci landed in China. And one of the most celebrated names in missionary annals, Bartholomew de Las Casas, belongs to the first half of this century.

Portugal of all lands or islands which had been, or might be, discovered between Cape Bojador and the East Indies, and granted at the same time a plenary indulgence for the souls of all who might perish in the prosecution of an enterprise calculated to rescue those extensive regions from the hands of infidels and pagans." Cooley's *Maritime and Inland Discovery*, Vol. I. p. 355.

[1] See Helps, *Spanish Conquest in America*, Vol. I. pp. 76, 77.

In the seventeenth century "the Jesuits sent many missionaries to the East Indies, to Tonquin, Bengal, Madura, the coast of Coromandel and Surat, with but moderate success[1]." Roman Catholic missionaries also laboured among the Chippeways, Mohawks, and other tribes of North American Indians. Perhaps the most noted mission in this century was that of the Jesuits in Paraguay. The Brazil missionaries, too, continued their labours, and "as early as 1683 there were fifty-six thousand baptized Indians on the banks of the upper Marânon[2]." We come now to the commencement of Protestant missionary efforts. In 1620 the 'Mayflower' arrived at New Plymouth, and "in the year 1646 the General Court of Massachusetts passed an act encouraging the propagation of the Gospel among the Indians[3]." The celebrated Eliot, who was called 'the Apostle of the Indians,' laboured for forty or fifty years in North America in the latter half of this century. In the other hemisphere, the Dutch, to whom the Portuguese colonies in Ceylon had been ceded, had the opportunity of prosecuting the work of missions among the natives of that island. This they did with much nominal, but little real, success[4].

Early in the eighteenth century the Danish mission to Tranquebar commenced a work in South India which laid the foundations of the extensive success

---

[1] *English Cyclopædia*, Art. 'Missions.'

[2] Markham's *Valley of the Amazons*, quoted in *From Pole to Pole: a Handbook of Missions*, Ch. VI.

[3] *From Pole to Pole*, Ch. V.   [4] See below, pp. 16—19.

which has since crowned the Church of England missions in that country. Ziegenbalg, Plutschau, ánd, most of all, Swartz, are honoured names in connexion with the Danish mission[1]. The Rev. J. Kiernander was the first Protestant missionary to Bengal. He had taken charge of the Cuddalore mission in 1740, but in 1758 he removed to Calcutta. There was not much progress, however, in missionary operations in the north of India until the establishment of the Baptist mission at Serampore at the end of the century.

One of the most interesting facts in reference to missionary enterprise during the eighteenth century is the extraordinary activity of the small body of Moravians. "It is worthy of particular observation," says Dr Brown[2], "that when the Moravians sent forth their first missionaries the congregation consisted of only six hundred persons, most of whom were poor despised exiles, yet...in the short period of eight or nine years they sent missionaries to Greenland, to St Thomas, Surinam, Berbice, the Indians of North America, to the negroes of South Carolina, to Lapland, to Tartary, to Guinea, to the Cape of Good Hope, and to the island of Ceylon."

---

[1] In the year 1709 the first contribution of the English was sent to the Indian mission. "Twenty pounds and a case of books were sent from the Society for the Propagation of the Gospel." The Society for Promoting Christian Knowledge took charge of the Danish mission in 1709-10 until 1824, when the mission was taken up by the Society for Propagating the Gospel in Foreign Parts.

[2] *History of Propagation of Christianity.*

The close of the eighteenth century witnessed a remarkable outburst of missionary zeal and enthusiasm in England, which may be traced to the growth of spiritual religion, consequent on the labours of Whitfield and Wesley. The 'Evangelical Movement' which began with methodism saved the nation from lapsing into infidelity, awaked the dormant energies of the Church of England, and brought into vigorous action aspirations after the extension of Christ's kingdom which soon bore fruit in the very large and decided increase of missionary efforts by which the nineteenth century has been characterized. It would be needless to particularize all the different missions which have been set on foot since the foundation of the Wesleyan Missionary Society in 1786, the London Missionary Society in 1795, and the Church Missionary Society in 1799. Suffice it to say that at the present time there is hardly a single portion of the globe where some efforts have not been made to sow the good seed of the Word of God. In Africa, west, south, and east; in India and Ceylon, Burmah and China; among the Red Indians of North America, the negroes of the West Indies, the Esquimaux of Greenland and Labrador, and the Indian tribes of South America; amid the natives of New Zealand, and in the 'many-islanded' Pacific, we may track the footsteps of those who bring good tidings of good, and publish salvation. That the efforts made are very inadequate to the results aimed at—that the labourers are, even now, very few, though the harvest truly is plenteous—that the work done is but a feeble and limited instrumentality is true enough. And sad it is that such should be the case: sad, too, that there should be among professed Christians persons who are not ashamed to taunt the supporters of missionary work with the little success which has been obtained[1]; saddest of all to reflect that the more rapid and complete diffusion of Christianity which might by this time have been achieved, has been hindered by the indifference and irreligion of Christians themselves. The object of this essay will be to show that the obstacles which have arisen to missionary success among the heathen from the side of Christians themselves have been many and great; and that if Christians had been more earnest, more honest, and more consistent in acting up to the principles of their holy religion, there would have not been the reason which there now is to lament for the little progress which has been made in the great work of evangelizing the world.

[1] *Little* it is, absolutely; but relatively to the amount of labour and expense employed it has not been little. What is most to be wished for is that a fitter proportion of Christians' wealth, and a larger amount of Christian interest should be given to what should surely be considered by Christians a great and glorious undertaking.

CHAPTER II.

OBSTACLES TO MISSIONARY SUCCESS.

It is a difficult matter rightly to classify the obstacles which have hindered the success of missionary work among the heathen, in consequence of the defective moral and religious condition of the very persons whose religious creed the heathen were invited to adopt. Yet without such classification this essay would become a mere compilation of testimonies drawn from missionary records bearing upon the subject. The hindrances to the successful prosecution of missionary work which we have now to consider have been mainly produced by causes external to the missions: but our view of the impediments which are owing to the unchristian conduct of Christians in their intercourse with the heathen will not be complete unless we also take notice of the moral and religious defects which have characterized some of the methods of missionary work, and have almost deprived them of their claim to be reckoned as missionary work at all. We shall have, then, to consider what, viewing the matter from the missionary side, we may call *Internal* and *External* Obstacles: and the subject of this chapter will fall under two main divisions: viz.

I. Hindrances arising from unchristian methods of missionary work.

II. Hindrances arising from unchristian conduct on the part of those professed Christians with whom the heathen have had intercourse.

I.

The only true method of missionary work is *moral suasion*. "Go ye into all the world, and *disciple* all nations." "Go into all the world and *proclaim the glad tidings* to all creation." "Ye shall be *witnesses* unto me both in Jerusalem, and in Judæa, and Samaria, and unto the ends of the earth[1]." Such are the commands of Christ. There is a message to be delivered. It is to be given to men in its simplicity. No force and no fraud may be used without contradicting the very purport and significance of the message itself. The consequences of its acceptance and rejection rest with God. Neither bribes nor penalties are warranted in the promulgation of Christ's gospel. For the faith without which it cannot be accepted consists in a willing submission of the heart and understanding to a Divine Revelation of God's nature and doings,—and not in an unwilling or unintelligent conformity to ecclesiastical systems or ceremonies.

Now there are three methods of propagating Christianity which stand out in the history of Missions as unmistakeably antagonistic to the only true and Chris-

---

[1] Matt. xxvi. 19; Mark xvi. 15; Acts i. 18.

tian method. These we may term the coercive method, the political method, and the 'accommodation' method.

Section I.

The operation of the coercive method may be seen in early European history, as in the wars of Charlemagne with the pagan Saxons. It received a mighty impulse in the Crusades, when the idea of fighting against the infidels became the highest object of chivalrous aspirations. Nor had its employment ceased in the earlier portion of the period of history with which our essay is concerned. Indeed, the view of missions prevalent among the successive companies of adventurers who left Portugal and Spain in the fifteenth and sixteenth centuries, to traverse the ocean in search of new lands and new wealth, was that of a holy war, a conquest of new domains for the Catholic Church. The Moors had been expelled from Spain, and the warfare with these enemies of the faith had ended. But extended navigation now opened the way for "a kind of crusade into splendid and unknown regions of infidels[1]." The conquest and the conversion of heathen tribes were regarded by many at that time as almost synonymous terms. The natives were to be *made* Christians. Subjected to the yoke of a foreign invader, they were by the same process to be brought under the yoke of Christ! Strange mixture of the earthly with the heavenly, of "the things which are Cæsar's" with

[1] Prescott.

": the things which are God's"! Yet who can be surprised that such sentiments should prevail among Roman Catholics, when the Pope of Rome could claim, and exercise, without dispute, the right as Head of the Church to make a grant of all newly-discovered countries to sovereigns who acknowledged his supremacy? The proclamations used by the Spanish conquerors in America proceeded upon the assumption "that to Jesus Christ all power was given in heaven and earth, and that this power devolved upon the Pope; who accordingly possessed authority in every land, not only for the preaching of the gospel, but also for compelling men to obey the law of nature[1]." The invaders were instructed to declare to the natives of the countries which they invaded the principal doctrines of the Christian faith; "to acquaint them, in particular, with the supreme jurisdiction of the Pope over all the kingdoms of the earth; to inform them of the grant which the holy Pontiff had made of their country to the King of Spain," and then to require their adoption of the Spaniards' religion, and their submission to the Spanish king. If the natives refused to comply, fire and sword were to be used to compel them[2].

That such a method of propagating Christianity

[1] Sepulveda, in his treatise *De Justis Belli Causis*, quoted by Helps in his *Spanish Conquest in America*, Vol. IV. p. 320. See, also, Helps' account (in the same chapter) of the discussion at Valladolid between Sepulveda and Las Casas.

[2] Robertson's *America*, Bk. III. Compare Pizarro's threatening message to Atabuallpa; and the oration of Father Vicente at his interview with the Inca (Helps, Vol. III. p. 516, 532 ff.). See Appendix, Note A.

was opposed to the very truth and substance of Christianity is evident. Nor could the heathen have been favourably inclined to embrace the religion of men whose first act was to deprive them of their lands and their liberty, and who required them to acknowledge an unknown earthly sovereign as the requisite preliminary to their worshipping the One True God, their unknown heavenly King. The pungent answer of the Caciques of Cenu to "the Bachiller Enciso," when he invaded their country and read the 'Requisition[1]' to them, shews the scornful opposition with which such unreasonable requirements might fairly be met. They replied to Enciso that what he said about one God seemed good to them, but that in what he "said about the Pope being the Lord of all the universe in the place of God and that he had given the land of the Indies to the king of Castille, the Pope must have been drunk when he did it, for he gave what was not his; also that the king who asked for, or received, this gift must be some madman, for that he asked to have that given him which belonged to others; and they added that should he come there to take it they would put his head on a stake. They were lords of this country, and there was no need of any other[2]."

[1] This remarkable document (El Requerimento) is quoted by Helps, Vol. I. 379: and is like the general form of proclamation alluded to by Robertson, as quoted above. (See Appendix, Note B.)

[2] Helps, Vol. I. 401, 402. Compare with this reply of the Caciques of Cenu that of the Inca Atahuallpa to Vicente de Valverde in which he drew a contrast between the messages of peace and brotherhood which had been previously sent to him and the present menace of fire and sword, &c. Helps, Vol. III. 540.

Altogether it is hardly too strong a way of stating the case to say that "the work of converting heathen people was at first undertaken in a barbarous spirit, and nominal conversions were often effected by the sword[1]."

There has been preserved a curious despatch from Columbus to the Court of Spain, in one paragraph of which "he boldly suggests that for the advantage of the souls of the cannibal Indians *the more of them that could be taken the better*," and he advises "that caravels should be sent each year with necessary things and the cargoes be paid for in slaves taken from amongst the cannibals[2]." We may see from this proposal for the establishment of a slave trade as a branch of missionary work, what strange notions were entertained even by the most enlightened minds of that period in reference to the extension of the Christian religion.

The central idea of missionary enterprise as it was at first undertaken in connexion with maritime discovery was not the proclamation of the gospel, but the authority of the church. This fact, together with the high regard which was then paid to mere external communion with the church and to the administration of baptism[3], explains though it cannot justify the disregard of common fairness and honesty which characterized the efforts made to conquer heathen 'for their good[4].'

[1] *English Cyclopædia*, Art. "Missions."
[2] Helps, Vol. I. 135.   [3] See Helps, Vol. I. 28.
[4] See Bernardo de Mesa's opinion laid before the Spanish king with reference to the servitude of the Indians. Helps, Vol. I. 258 (See Appendix, Note C.).

Section II.

The most signal instance of another faulty method of missionary work calculated rather to hinder than to promote the extension of true religion is to be found in the history of the Dutch settlement in Ceylon. The Dutch in their attempts to christianise the natives depended too much on legislative enactments, and the enforcement upon the heathen of political tests. Baptism was made a civil distinction. It was the law "that none could inherit property but those who were baptized and registered[1]." The consequence of this political method of christianizing was that "there spread over the island an organized hypocrisy[2]." This was painfully evident, when, "on the accession of British rule, the natives were prepared to persevere in the same unsoundness of profession. The Singhalese brought their children in crowds to the ceremony of 'Christianikarenewa,' or Christian making. It had been declared honourable by the Portuguese to undergo such a ceremony [baptism]; it had been rendered profitable by the Dutch, and after 300 years' familiarity with the process the natives were unable to divest themselves of the belief that submission to the ceremony was enjoined by orders from the civil government[3]." Sir E. Tennent, in his *Christianity in Ceylon*, speaks of a body of 'Government Christians,' who with scarcely

---

[1] *Missionary Guide Book*, c. viii. § 4.
[2] *Church Missionary Intelligencer* (Aug. 1858).
[3] *Ibid.*

an exception are heathens or sceptics, and whose reckless and abandoned conduct proves a great obstacle to Christianity. This class is the product of the Dutch policy[1]. The same policy was followed in the islands of the Indian Archipelago with the same lamentable results, namely, a large number of nominal converts who on the first convenient opportunity relapsed into heathenism[2].

The evil effects of such a method of propagating Christianity are evident. How could truth and sincerity be expected on the part of the converts? When "proclamation was publicly made that no native could aspire to the rank of modliar, or be permitted to farm land or hold office under the government, who had not first undergone the ceremony of baptism, become a member of the Protestant church, and subscribed to the doctrines contained in the Helvetic confession of faith[3]," many natives of course came forward, promptly enough, "to exhibit themselves possessed of the necessary qualifications for office," and "made ready profession of Christianity." But what was their Christianity worth? and what must have been the impression left on their naturally suspicious minds? This system of political bribery, as Tennent calls it, was in reality no less a system of compulsion than the coercive

[1] Tennent's *Christianity in Ceylon*, pp. 85, &c.
[2] See Abeel's *Journal of a Residence in China*, p. 6. "Professing Christians were preferred to their heathen neighbours in the distribution of petty offices under government, and even a monthly allowance of rice was served out to those, and those only, who had received baptism."
[3] Tennent, p. 45.

method of fire and sword; not indeed so cruel, or so fatal to the temporal interests of those affected by it; but a system which from the very reason that it was more seductive was the further removed from that honest simplicity with which Christian truth should be commended to the consciences of men. And when the natives saw that government pressure, as they might call it, was put upon them to induce an immediate adoption of a foreign creed, the nature of which they could not be expected to understand, and the arguments for which they could not be expected to oppose, surely "they could not fail to conclude that there must be something defective or unreal in a religion" which required such means for its extension. However good the motive may have been, the Dutch made a serious mistake in adopting this policy: "it was tantamount to setting a premium on hypocrisy[1]." The ecclesiastical records of the Dutch in Ceylon contain an expression of the conviction felt by the Dutch ministers themselves, that large numbers of the converts were merely nominal, their profession unsound, and the converts themselves *sine Christo Christiani*[2]. Reference has been already made to the large class of unsatisfactory so-called Christians which sprang up in consequence of this political method of missionary work. One of the greatest obstacles which has deterred the Singhalese from seeking Christianity, since the British rule commenced on the island, is, we are

---

[1] Hough's *History of Christianity in India*, Vol. III. p. 93.
[2] Tennent, p. 65.

told on good authority[1], "the apprehension of being identified by their conversion with a class whose reputation and whose practice are alike an outrage on the religion in which they were born, and an insult to that which they profess to have adopted."

Section III.

The 'accommodation' to the prejudices of the heathen, which has given its name to the strange system of missionary operations which we have now to consider, was used extensively by the Jesuits, especially in India and China; and was the source of much dispute between their order and the Dominicans, Capuchins, and other missionaries who—sometimes from jealousy of the success of Jesuit missionaries, sometimes also, it is to be hoped, from a regard for the truth and honour of Christianity—objected very strenuously to "the mixture of heathen and Christian elements" in the Jesuits' method of teaching[2]. The most remarkable exhibition of the system is to be found in the history of the Madura mission[3]. Robert de Nobili, who was the founder of the mission, having qualified himself for the task by a diligent study of the native languages, pretended to be a Brahman from the

---

[1] Tennent, p. 90.

[2] See Kurz, *History of Christian Church*, Vol. II. §§ 35. 3; 45. 3. (T. & T. Clark, Edinburgh). Dubois, *Letters on the State of Christianity in India*, L. I. p. 7.

[3] So contrary are the deceit and intrigue manifested in the history of this Mission, that the Historian of Christianity in India almost feels bound to apologize for introducing it. (See Hough, II. 218.)

West; and he with his colleagues entered upon a marvellous labour of deception[1], with "the determination to become all things to all men for the accomplishment of their object; withholding till some more favourable time the inculcation of Christian simplicity, and adopting, in the interim, almost without qualification, the practices of heathenism[2]." In most vivid contrast with the simplicity which had characterised the labours of Xavier is the tortuous policy of Nobili and his followers. He had done little, they thought, to penetrate into the ranks of heathenism, but they would do more. He had offended the prejudices of the Hindu by preaching to the poor and oppressed, the Pariah and the outcast; they (forgetful of one great sign of the truth of Christianity, that "to the poor the Gospel is preached") would ingratiate themselves with the proud and haughty Brahman. And so they adopted the clothing, the habits, the food of the Brahmans. They announced themselves as Brahmans from the West; they did not scruple to employ forgery and perjury in order to substantiate their claims[3]. They went about clothed in the sacred yellow robe; they bore the sacred spot of sandalwood-paste upon their foreheads; they wore the wooden shoe; they religiously abstained from meat and intoxicating liquors; they religiously per-

---

[1] See Steinmetz, *History of the Jesuits*, Vol. III. 491. The lives of the Jesuit missionaries, says the Rev. W. S. Mackay, quoted in Steinmetz, "were but one long, persevering, toilsome LIE."

[2] Tennent's *Christianity in Ceylon*, p. 16.

[3] See Hough, II. 231. Steinmetz, Vol. III. 378.

formed the requisite ablutions; and "affected to spurn the Pariahs and lower castes[1]." They incorporated heathen customs into the ceremonies of the Romish Church until the only distinction between a procession of 'Christians' and a procession of heathen was that the image of the Virgin took the place of the idol Vishnu or Siva upon the sacred car! "There was the same noise of trumpets, and taum-taums, and kettledrums; there was the same blaze of rockets, and Roman candles, and blue lights; there were the same dancers with the same marks of sandalwood and vermilion on their naked bodies. The new Christianity of Madura disguised itself as adroitly as the priests who taught it. They married children with all the silly observances of Paganism, and buried the dead with all its ghastly superstitions[2]."

Thousands of converts are said to have been made by the Jesuits in South India; but, when Pope Benedict XIV. in 1704, issued a rigorous bull condemning "all the superstitious practices till then tolerated by

---

[1] Tennent, p. 17. Comp. Juvenci, in Steinmetz, Vol. III. 381 (note). "Il ne faut pas qu'ils puissent dire: il vient encore nous prêcher le Dieu des Pariahs."

[2] Kaye's *Christianity in India*, p. 33. Kaye says, "It may be questioned whether the Jesuit missionaries themselves were not the only real converts. It is almost enough to say of the scandalous nature of their proceedings that they brought a blush to the hard cheek of Menezes."

For an account of one of these processions, see *Calcutta Review*, quoted by Tennent, p. 18 (note), and Hough, II. 428, 429. Steinmetz, III. 483—485. (These passages will be found below in the Appendix, Note D.)

the missionaries," conversions ceased; and when, at last, the Hindus found out that these foreign teachers were only disguised 'Feringhis' (Europeans), and were fellow-countrymen with the French and English who in the 18th century invaded their country, "apostacy became general, and Christianity became more and more an object of contempt and aversion in proportion as the European manners became better known to the Hindoos[1]." When the imposture had become a thoroughly recognized fact amongst the natives, what a monstrous obstacle would it place in the way of true missionary success! No sincere and honest inquirer after truth would be satisfied; and those who were not such inquirers, although they might not receive any moral shock when they discovered the deceit that had been practised by the missionaries, and might rather applaud the ingenuity shown, would be encouraged in their indifference to real religious truth; that indifference which is the very essence and characteristic of ceremonial Hinduism.

The temporising policy of the Jesuits was as opposed to the truthfulness of the Gospel as their adoption of the Brahmanistic status was to the humility of the Gospel[2]. And this 'accommodation' theory,

---

[1] Abbé Dubois, *Letters*, &c. pp. 11, 12.

[2] For an answer to the plea of the Jesuits that accommodation to heathen prejudices was indispensable to the success of missionary work, see Hough's *Reply to Abbé Dubois*, pp. 68 ff. Compare Cardinal Bellarmine's remark condemning the conduct of his nephew Nobili. Cahours says that Bellarmine wrote his nephew "a letter full of reproaches," and unhesitatingly condemned his conduct. He considered that to

as might reasonably be expected, led to the degradation of the Christian missionary instead of to the elevation of the heathen inquirer. Mr Hough[1] once asked a priest on the Coromandel coast by what scriptural authority they performed the ceremony of the Rutt[2], and other idolatrous customs. He replied, "There is no authority for it in Scripture, *but if you come amongst dogs you must do as dogs do!*"

The character of the converts thus made could hardly be expected to stand very high. Nor need we be surprised to find among such converts "nothing else but *a vain phantom* of Christianity, without any real or practical faith[3]." How could it be otherwise? These missionaries, afraid to proclaim the honest truth and boldly confront the falsehood and pride of Brahmanism, depending for their success upon an "unscriptural policy and shameful compromise of everything resembling the pure and undefiled religion of the New Testament[4];" glorying in the devices of human wit instead of bearing the reproach of Christ's

---

imitate the Brahmans and to observe heathen rites was opposed to the humility of Christ and very dangerous to the faith. *Minus quidem est*, he says, *ut Brachmani non convertantur ad fidem quam ut Christiani non libere et sincere Evangelium prædicent.* (Steinmetz, Vol. III. 383.)

[1] *Reply to Dubois*, p. 82.

[2] The "Rathan" or "Tér," as it is called in S. India, is the sacred car on which the idols are placed, when the priests and worshippers go in procession. The Romanists use this sacred car in exactly the same way as the heathen, with the exception that the images are images of the Virgin Mary and Saints instead of being representations of Vishnu, Siva, Kali, and other heathen deities. See Hough's *Reply*, p. 83.

[3] Dubois' *Letters, &c.* p. 73.   [4] Hough's *Reply*, p. 85.

Gospel; degrading the truth of Christianity even in the eyes of their Roman Catholic brethren—how could these men expect to find sincerity, stedfastness, or "practical faith" in their converts?

A similar "religious policy" to that adopted in India was followed by the Jesuits in China. They "allowed their converts there to retain many of their idolatrous superstitions; and while they took away from them some of their clay-gilt gods they substituted in their stead the images of the Virgin, &c., and relics of saints[1]." The Jesuits, in opposition to Dominicans and Franciscans, maintained that the Chinese ceremonies in honour of the dead were civil, and not religious, rites[2]: and thus defended their toleration of what by less subtle minds were at once recognized and condemned as heathenish practices. These "Chinese customs" were condemned by the Papal see at the same time when the proceedings of the Jesuits in India were forbidden[3].

We have said enough to shew that the cause of Christianity in the world has been injured even by some of the methods adopted to propagate it, because those methods themselves have been wanting in the

[1] *Missionary Guide-Book*, p. 229.
[2] Medhurst's *China, its State and Prospects*, Ch. ix.
[3] Steinmetz (III. 509) speaks of the favour with which the Jesuits looked upon the Chinese system, and says of one of their altars "lately discovered at Shanghai," an engraving of which he gives, "It certainly very emphatically attests the extent to which the accommodating Jesuits engrafted their religion on that of the pagans—on their very altar of sacrifice uniting the heathen symbol of the Dragon and the Spirit of Fire with the Cross, the I. H. S. and nails of the Company."

essential qualifications of justice, sincerity, and truth. Physical force, political expediency, 'pious frauds,'— these are weapons which only recoil against those who use them; they are forged on human anvils, and have never proved mighty in God's sight, whatever they have appeared to men, for the pulling down of the strongholds of error and sin[1]. Men may be forced, or cajoled, or deceived, into the profession of Christianity, but the possession of it can only be acquired by a diviner and more spiritual method[2].

II.

We proceed now to consider the hindrances which the unchristian conduct of nominal Christians has placed in the way of missionary success.

The three things which, considered in connexion with the subject of religion, form the most important features of the history of the world's progress, are conquest, commerce, and colonization. And these three, with the blended good and evil occasioned by them, have all

[1] τὰ γὰρ ὅπλα ἡμῶν τῆς στρατείας οὐ σαρκικὰ ἀλλὰ δυνατὰ τῷ Θεῷ πρὸς καθαίρεσιν ὀχυρωμάτων. κ.τ.λ. (2 Cor. x. 4.)

[2] The Romanist method and means of converting the heathen (not only among the Jesuits but generally,) partook more of the *mechanical* than of the *moral* element of missionary work. See, for instance, a description of proselytizing by the Spaniards in California (1767) in the *Church Missionary Intelligencer*, Oct. 1858. Compare the account of the baptism of Juan Gigante on Magellan's vessel (Cooley, Vol. II. 48), and the remarks of Robertson (*America*, Book VIII.). Southey, in his *Life of Wesley*, relates that an Indian chief Tonochichi said to Wesley, "We would not be made Christians as the Spaniards make Christians, *we would be taught* before we are baptized." See also Southey's *History of Brazil*, Ch. VIII. Steinmetz, III. 408, 504. (Some of the passages referred to will be found in Appendix, Note E.)

contributed to the development of that international life, or interdependence of one people upon another, which though always in some degree operative within smaller spheres of action and intercourse, has, since the period of the Reformation, gradually extended itself to the remotest regions of the globe. This development of mutual intercourse, like all processes of human thought and action, has borne within itself sources of weakness as well as of strength, seeds of error as well as of truth, occasions for the exhibition of the evil, as well as of the nobler, side of human nature. Conquest has not contented itself with such a subjugation to law of previously uncivilized tribes as might form the basis of national expansion and elevation[1]: but the lust of power has given rise to pride and cruelty. Commerce has not always been, as it ought to be, doubly beneficial, (like Mercy, blessing him who gives, and him who takes):' but the greed of gain has produced a fearful amount of fraud and injustice. Colonization has never proved an unmixed good for the land in which new settlements have been made: but amid the benefits of mutual intercourse the 'vices of civilization' have reproduced themselves in another soil, often inoculating a new race with a hitherto unknown poison. And when the oppressive conqueror, the fraudulent and grasping

[1] Nihil ad posteros gloriosius nec honorificentius transmitti potest quam barbaros domare rudes et paganos ad vitæ civilis societatem revocare efferos in gyrum rationis reducere hominisque atheos et a Deo alienos divini numinis reverentia imbuere. Hakluyt, quoted by Anderson, *History of the Colonial Church*, Vol. I. p. 159 (note) (2d Ed.).

merchant, and the irreligious colonist, have been, by profession, *Christians*, it may be seen at once how huge an obstacle the conduct of such persons would raise to the praiseworthy efforts of the Christian missionary.

In correspondence with what has been said we shall endeavour to view the obstacles to missionary success under three aspects; namely, obstacles of *Oppression;* obstacles of *Avarice;* and obstacles of *Evil Example.* The division of the subject is only a rough one, and it will be easily seen that the demarcations of the three classes are not very distinct; but they are sufficiently so to make the discussion of the subject more lucid than it would be if we contented ourselves with a simple chronological or geographical arrangement. In the first section we shall consider the treatment of heathen by European conquerors; in the second, the opposition which the greed and rapacity of traders has offered to missionary efforts; and in the third, the shameful hindrances which the ill-conduct of Europeans in heathen countries has presented to the successful progress of the missionary work.

Section I. Conquerors.

1. We have already seen that the theory of the earliest missions from Europe to the heathen nations in the newly-discovered regions of the world was based upon the idea of conquest. But there were far worse hindrances to the success of missions among the heathen than a faulty and unjust theory. A study of the manner in which the Portuguese and Spanish expeditions

to America and India were conducted, and of the conduct of most of those who conducted them, leads us to the conclusion that, however grand the public professions which were made of subserving the cause of Christianity by the subjugation of barbarous nations to the Cross of Christ, and however sincere on the part of a few enlightened individuals such professions might have been, there was but little real Christianity at all among those bands of adventurers who in search of fame or wealth left Europe for the Indies, East and West.

Of the cruelties of the Spaniards in the West Indies and on the 'Terra Firma' of America, and of the consequent abhorrence in which their name was held by the native tribes, let the famous Bishop of Chiapa—the earnest, eloquent, and indefatigable 'Protector of the Indians'—speak. He says[1] that the advent of the Spaniards to the Indian tribes of the American islands and continent was like the assault of hungry tigers, wolves, and lions upon gentle lambs; that the Spaniards, 'who boasted themselves of being Christians,' employed themselves in destroying the Indians by cruel wars and unjust and savage slavery; and he applies to them the words in Zechariah[2], "Feed the flock of slaughter, *whose possessors slay them, and hold themselves not guilty; and*

---

[1] My quotations from Las Casas are taken from a Latin translation of his *Destruction of the Indies*, dedicated to Frederic IV., Count Palatine. This Latin translation is entitled *Crudelitates Hispanorum in Indiis Patratæ*. My references are to the pages of this Edition. I have also consulted a French version, edited at Amsterdam, 1698.

[2] xi. 4, 5.

they that sell them say, Blessed be the Lord, for I am rich."

The accounts which Las Casas gives of the inhuman tortures inflicted upon the poor Indians, and of the reckless conduct of the Spaniards, are enough to make the reader shudder with horror at the deeds of the 'Christians,' and weep for pity at the sufferings of the 'heathen.' And, according to the good bishop's testimony, the inducement to the perpetration of all this cruelty was the lust of power and of gold. "This it was," says he, "which made the Spaniards treat the natives, as he himself an eyewitness can testify, he will not say as beasts—he wished it had been even this—but as the very filth of the earth[1]."

The narrative of the Cuban cacique, Hathuey, has been often quoted as an evidence of the abhorrence excited among the native Indians by the avarice and cruelty of the Spaniards. Mr Helps gives the story thus[2]: "As for any inducements which the Spanish religion held out to the Indians, we may judge how far these were understood or estimated by the story of Hathuey, cacique of a part of Cuba, who had spies at Hispaniola to keep him informed of the proceedings of the Spaniards there. He was in apprehension that they would come, as they afterwards did, to his territory; so calling his people together, and recounting the cruelties of the Spaniards, he said that they did

[1] Las Casas, p. 8.
[2] *Spanish Conquest in America*, Vol. I. p. 199. (Las Casas, pp. 22, 23).

all these things for a great lord whom they loved much, which lord he would now show them. Accordingly he produced a small basket filled with gold. 'Here is the lord whom they serve, and after whom they go, and as you have heard they are already longing to pass over to this place not pretending more than to seek this lord; wherefore let us make to him here a festival and dances, so that when they come he may tell them to do us no harm.' The Indians approved this counsel, and danced round the gold until they were exhausted, when the cacique turned to them and said they should not keep the god of the Christians anywhere; for were it even in their entrails it would be torn out, but that they should throw it into the river that the Christians might not know where it was. 'And so,' says the account, 'they threw it.'" This same cacique was afterwards conquered and sentenced to be burnt alive. When he was at the stake, a Franciscan monk used the time which was allowed him by the executioners in persuading Hathuey to adopt the Christian faith, saying that eternal glory would be his, if he believed, but if not, eternal punishment. After Hathuey had thought a little, he asked the monk whether the gate of heaven would be open to the Spaniards. The monk replied that it would be to the good Spaniards. The cacique without further hesitation said that he had no wish to go to heaven, but would rather go to hell lest he should be in the same abode with that cruel race[1].
"This," adds the indignant narrator, "is the kind of

[1] Las Casas, pp. 23, 24.

honour which is paid to God and our holy faith by the Spaniards in America."

Another narrative of Las Casas furnishes, perhaps, still more striking evidence of the hindrance to missionary work which arose from the reckless conduct of the Spaniards. It is an account of what took place in Yucatan. Four Franciscan monks, who were received into the country on the express condition that they should come by themselves, and not be accompanied by the Spaniards (whom the natives looked upon as almost a different race from the missionaries who treated them kindly), had made some progress in the conversion of the natives to Christianity. The idols had been burnt. The children were under Christian instruction. Neighbouring tribes came in, and voluntarily (a thing unheard of before) submitted themselves to the Spanish rule. The joy and hope of the monks, Las Casas tells us, were now great. But "lo! by some other way eighteen Spanish horsemen and twelve foot-soldiers came into the country, bringing with them many loads of idols which they had taken in other countries. The captain of the Spaniards summoned a chief of the province into which they had entered, and bade him take these idols and distribute them through his own territory; and that an Indian man or woman was to be given in exchange for each idol: otherwise he would make war against him." The terrified chief did so, and the Indians gave up their children: "he who had two, one; and he who had three, two: and so was transacted this sacrilegious bargain, and the cacique managed to satisfy those—I will not call them Christians, but—Spaniards." The narrator then mentions the death of Juan Garcia, one of these "sacrilegious robbers," and tells us that Garcia's last act was to enforce upon an Indian attendant that the idols under his bed were very good ones, and that the price she was to ask for them must not be less than an Indian for each. Las Casas concludes his account with indignant irony. "Let persons now reflect what sort of progress in religion is made, and what sort of examples of Christianity the Spaniards set when they go to America, with what honour they glorify God, and how earnestly they strive that he should be worshipped by these infidels[1]."

In this and in several instances the conduct of the marauding Spaniards gave the death-blow to missionary efforts which had been peacefully begun, and were being hopefully prosecuted. And we are not surprised that the Protector of the Indians, in his scheme for a colony which he attempted to found on the Pearl coast, should stipulate that no Spaniard should be allowed to enter it; nor that, afterwards, when setting on foot the Dominican mission into the 'Tierra del Guerra[2],' he should make it part of the compact between himself and the Spanish authorities that no Spaniard under heavy penalties, except the Governor [of Guatemala]

---

[1] Las Casas, pp. 61—63.

[2] By this mission he undertook to bring into peaceable condition the Indians of that territory, who were much dreaded by the Spaniard colonists in the neighbourhood. From the success of the missionaries the land gained the name of *Vera Paz*.

himself, should be allowed for five years to enter into the territory[1].

It is most condemnatory of the conduct of the Spanish colonists, and most evidential of the hindrances which their unchristian conduct raised against missionary work, that they left no stone unturned in opposing the disinterested and beneficent efforts made in favour of the oppressed Indians by Las Casas and like-minded men. And the inoffensive and well-meaning missionaries were sometimes, as at Cumana and in Florida, put to death by the Indians because of the treachery and cruelty of their Spanish fellow-countrymen[2].

The natural and persistent antagonism which must ever exist between the injustice of all systems of slavery and the gentleness and humanity of the Christian religion has never been more strikingly instanced than in the history of the life of Bartholomew de Las Casas[3]. His efforts to ameliorate the condition of the oppressed Indians, his bold and fervent advocacy of their cause by mouth and pen, his personal labours amongst them, his unwearied and enlightened opposition to the evils of the *repartimiento* (or *encomienda*) system, throw a bright light into the otherwise dark and gloomy picture of the

[1] Helps, Vol. III. 337.
[2] See the spirited justification of the Indians by Las Casas, when opposing Sepulveda, who had brought forward the death of Father Luis Cancer as an evidence that the Indians should be converted by forcible and not by peaceable means. Helps, Vol. IV. 334, 335. (The passage is given below in Appendix, Note F.)
[3] For an interesting account of the beginning of this great and good man's career of philanthropic and missionary labour, see Helps, Vol. I. pp. 465 ff.

Spanish conquests in America. The Spaniards would not follow his example in freeing the Indian slaves who had been allotted to him, and would not listen to the Christian advice which from that time forward he did not cease to give both to the government at home and to the colonists in the Indies, but preferred the possession of slaves to the practice and propagation of Christian truth,—and so the establishment and success of missions was impeded, the newly-conquered countries were often made desolate, and the whole state of affairs in the western possessions of the court of Spain became a disgrace to the name of Christians. The colonists were actually glad when a revolt among the Indians occurred, so that they had the prospect of a fresh supply of slaves. All the kind intentions of Queen Isabella were frustrated. The condition of Christianizing the natives attached to the *encomienda*, in virtue of which a Spaniard became an owner of so many Indians, was treated as a mere formality[1]. It was in vain that the good Dominicans (who seemed to have been far tenderer to heathen than their brethren had been to heretics on this side of the Atlantic[2]) protested, and preached in 'very piercing and terrible words,' and pleaded the cause of the unfortunate Indians. The lordly Spaniard must be served, and what were these poor wretches good for else? The laws of Burgos (1512)

---

[1] Helps, Vol. I. 188, 197, 213.

[2] Prescott says that they " devoted themselves to the good work of conversion in the new world with the same zeal that they showed for persecution in the old."

were a well-intentioned effort on the part of the Spanish home-government to control the rapacity and cruelty of the colonists: but when conduct like that of Ovando in the case of the princess Anacaona, or of Vasco Nuñez in the case of the cacique Careta[1], was considered legitimate and praiseworthy by the leaders of military expeditions, it was not likely that laws the basis of which was the retention of the system of *encomiendas*,—whereby the enslavement of Indians was warranted and sanctioned as a legal and just act,—would form any barrier to the cruelty and tyranny of these 'Christian' conquerors. And what hope was there that the natives, with such an exhibition of Christianity before them, would be ready to listen to the missionary monks who spoke to them of the religion of peace and love? Must we not rather concur with the melancholy observations of the historian when he comments on the reasonable aversion of Indians to the society of Spaniards: "What peace, what love, what beauty or holiness of life did they see amongst the Spaniards that should have tempted any sane Indian to take up his abode amongst these new men, especially if his companionship was only to be some form of servitude?... The implements, dress, and toys of the new comers may have had some attraction for the Indians, but surely not enough to conquer their *reasonable distaste for Spanish bloodhounds*[2]." Before these Christian conquerors came the Indians had been free, now they were slaves; before,

---

[1] Helps, I. 207, 341 (see Appendix, Note G).
[2] Helps, I. 198, 199.

they had enjoyed their own method of an easy, wandering life,—now they were worked to death in hard labour for cruel and inconsiderate masters; then they had been sufficiently provided with the necessaries and even with some of the luxuries of life[1], but now "the white man had penetrated into their land, avarice and pride and ambition and sordid care and pining labour were soon to follow, and the indolent paradise of the Indian was about to disappear for ever[2]." A new religion, indeed, was offered, which spake of high hopes and a lofty destiny for men, and of a Saviour from sin and death. But offered, how? sometimes at the point of the sword, sometimes by more peaceable methods, but never exhibited in the fulness and freedom of its truth, and almost always contradicted and set at nought by the majority of those who professed it.

Even the formality of the proclamation, which has been mentioned before in this Essay[3], was evaded; and the Spaniards were wont to read the invitation to the natives to become Christians "to themselves and the trees" in the middle of the night, in some forest, previous to a furious onslaught in the morning upon some unfortunate Indian village, the inhabitants of which, asleep when the requisition to acknowledge God, the Pope, and the King of Castile, had been furtively read (not without a mocking laughter, we may well suppose, among the Christian soldiery), were awakened by the war-cry of these strange crusaders, to find out how evil

[1] Helps, I. 198.
[2] Irving, in *Life and Voyages of Columbus*.
[3] pp. 13, 14.

a thing it was to be 'infidels,' but surely not to discover that it was a good thing to be 'Christians[1].'

2. If we turn now to contemplate the missionary efforts made in connexion with the Portuguese conquests in India[2], we shall find that they were perverted and impeded by the same spirit of proud contempt for the rights of mankind which characterised the predatory invaders of Cuba, Mexico, or Peru. The treatment of the Syrian native Christians on the Malabar coast (a history of which would of itself occupy a volume[3]), the establishment and proceedings of the Inquisition at Goa, and the general arrogance of the Portuguese in their dealings with the natives, were not calculated to commend Christianity to the Hindús or Musalmáns who observed these things. There is both Portuguese and native testimony to "the tyrannies, robberies, and all sorts of insolence[4]" whereby the Portuguese in India rendered the Christian name odious to the surrounding heathen and Muhammed-

---

[1] "The name of Christianity was made familiar to the natives, but it was to them a terrible name.... It must have seemed to them the revelation of some monstrous Moloch, more horrible because more widely and indiscriminately destructive than any war god of their own." Howitt's *Colonization and Christianity*, p. 119.

[2] The Portuguese acquisitions of power and territory in Africa were connected with the slave-trade, which is noticed in another part of this section. And their conquests in Brazil present a similar picture of violence and cruelty to that presented by the Spaniards in the other parts of South America.

[3] Kaye mentions it as "that great struggle to which Gibbon has devoted two pregnant pages, and Hough more than a volume of his work." *Christianity in India*, p. 23.

[4] See Manuel de Faria, cited by Hough, I. 263, and Howitt, Ch. XIII.

ans[1]. A remarkable rebuke was addressed to one of the viceroys of Goa by a Muhammedan prince, in which the Musalmán speaks thus to the Christian. After complaining of the forcible abduction of Muhammedan children from ships which touched at the Portuguese ports on the coast, he says: "This is a matter that I cannot but be extremely offended with, neither can I judge otherwise of your permitting such violences, but that you have a mind to break with me...I am confident that the King of Portugal will not thank any that shall be instrumental in making a breach between me and him by compelling my subjects thus against their wills to turn Christians, a practice that is abominable in the sight of all the world: nay, I am confident that Jesus Christ himself, the God whom you adore, cannot be well pleased with such service as this: force and compulsion in all such cases being what God, kings, and all the people of the world do abominate...I do therefore entreat you to see that this matter be speedily redressed, but especially that of taking people's children from them by violence, which is a thing I stand amazed at, and am in duty bound to see remedied[2]." This same prince, by name Hidalcaon, in a speech to "his captains," tells them that the Portuguese had come amongst them at first in the character of merchants, but instead of store-

---

[1] See a quotation in Hough from *Asiatic Researches*, giving an extract from an account written by a Muhammedan of the insolence and bigotry of the Portuguese. I. 264, 265.

[2] Geddes' *Short History of the Church of Malabar*, ("Done out of Portuguese into English." London, 1644) pp. 25, 26.

houses they built forts, and that it was now "more than time for the natives to look about them, and to join together to extirpate such cruel tyrants and ravagers of so many kingdoms and enemies to the general quiet and commerce of the world; and that for one thing especially, which was what no patience was able to endure, their compelling the Indians in all places, where they had power, to change their religion[1]."

The history from which the above extracts are taken goes on to speak of "*à la Dragoon* conversions," in which monks were priests one day and soldiers the next. One "famous Portuguese missionary," Fernando Vinagre, is mentioned by Portuguese writers as having, in a certain expedition against a native rájá, "behaved himself like a great captain and a great apostle, and to have appeared one day in armour and another in a surplice, and to have baptized several in his armour, with his surplice over it." An admiral who accompanied Vinagre is reckoned "as another St Paul in governing all that came under his power, both with his sword and with his voice: *a word and a voice*, say they, *worthy of a glorious eternity*[2]."

It was not likely that missions should succeed when carried on by such methods and in such a spirit as this. And even if amongst the friars, who accompanied the Portuguese soldiers and merchants to the East, there

---

[1] Geddes, pp. 26, 27.
[2] Geddes, p. 28. Steinmetz (*Hist. of Jesuits*, Book VII.) speaks of Goa as "the great stronghold of bayonet orthodoxy," and of the Portuguese as using "the apostolical musket in aid of the missionary scheme."

were some who were neither ambitious of military prowess nor content with monastic indolence[1], they could have had little chance of persuading the natives of India that the religion professed by such men as Albuquerque and his successors was a religion worth adopting. A bitter and indignant speech is recorded as having been made to the Portuguese by a native of the island of Ito, a person of some distinction named Gemulio. Upbraiding them for their treachery and cruelty, he continues, "You preach Christ crucified to us, and at the same time crucify those you have persuaded to believe in Him. You will make others to be Christians, without appearing to be such yourselves. You must know we are not ignorant of what you have done to the king of Xael, and how you rewarded his great kindness and civility to you with violences and outrages, and his subjects' good turns with dishonouring their wives: we know likewise how you have used the Queen of Aram, whom after she had lost both her kingdom and husband to secure you, you have dishonourably thrown off, as one who could be of no further use to you. Be gone therefore immediately out of this island, and hereafter do not presume to set your foot or so much as cast your eye upon it." The Portuguese historian who relates this adds the reflection,

---

[1] "It may be doubted whether the Franciscan friars who accompanied the Portuguese mariners to India did not for the most part suffer the missionary character to subside into the monastic. They established monasteries; they built churches; but they made few genuine converts." Kaye, p. 16.

"Thus we lose places by our insolences which we gained by our valour[1]."

3. We turn next, and with more of shame and sorrow, to the proceedings of English Protestants in North America. In the early expeditions of the English to America many outrages were committed against the native inhabitants of that country, although there were not lacking some amongst the explorers of that day who endeavoured, as far as they could, to teach the truth of the Gospel to the heathen[2]. When colonies had been planted in America the colonists often came into collision with the Indians; and these petty wars seem to have exhibited as much barbarity on the side of the English Christians as on the side of the Indian heathen; and they were often provoked by the deeds of violence and rapine perpetrated by the white men against the native tribes. "There is no darker page in the history of the nations of Europe," says the historian of our Church in the colonies, "than that which relates their oppression of the aboriginal inhabitants of countries which they have colonised. The tide of native life has been beaten back in well nigh every quarter into which the stream of her population has poured itself; and the swarthy savages of the west, of the east, of the south have alike withered, or are withering away, at the approach of the white man. The treatment of the Indian tribes of North America by the English settlers upon their lands presents no exception to this humi-

---

[1] Geddes, pp. 29, 30.
[2] See Anderson's *History of the Colonial Church*, I. 71.

liating story[1]." The greater part of the seventeenth century passed away in acts of mutual hostility between the native tribes and the English settlers; and no systematic effort was made by Protestant Christians to elevate or instruct the savages, with the exception of Eliot's mission in New England. Many professions that the extension of the English rule was made for the propagation of God's truth find place in the history of these settlements: but it rarely happened that the acts of the settlers agreed with the rules and principles by which they professed to be guided. Thus, for instance, the charter of Massachusetts described the principal end of the plantation to be that "our said People, Inhabitants there, may be soe religiously, peaceablie, and civilly governed, as their good Life and orderly Conversation maie wynn and incite the Natives of the Countrie to the knowledg and obedience of the onlie true God and Sauior of mankinde and the Christian Fayth[2]." And the device upon the seal of the colony was the figure of an Indian with a label at his mouth containing the words, "Come over and help us." The New England emigrants also drew up a covenant, in which they bound themselves to study the advancement of the Gospel, and not to lay a stumblingblock before any, "no, not the Indians whose good we desire to promote." But their actions consorted not with their words[3].

[1] Anderson, III. 287. [2] Cited by Anderson, II. 138.
[3] The historian of New England speaks of the settlers as devils incarnate, and declares that unless he had a pen made of a porcupine's

The iniquitous war with the Pequod Indians[1], whether it is to be attributed simply to the revengeful spirit, or, which seems probable, also to the fanaticism of the Connecticut colonists[2], is sufficient evidence that the contact between the Europeans and the Red Indians at that time was not of such a nature as to promote the cause of missions, but rather retarded and impeded, not only the prospect of their success, but the very possibility of their existence.

The labours of John Eliot, whose persevering zeal and undaunted faith have encouraged many a missionary since[3], and the self-denying and arduous toils of the French missionaries in Canada were, humanly speaking, but a feeble make-weight against the hindrances which the cruel and unjust behaviour of the European was heaping up against the progress of Christian truth among the Red Indians of North America.

It was an evil thing that Spanish and Portuguese invaders should be reckless of human rights; but it was more evil, because less excusable, that those who professed a purer form of religion, and made a boast that the individual conscience had rights and duties

---

quill and dipped in aquafortis, he could not describe all their cruelties. Howitt, p. 347.

[1] Howitt, p. 346.

[2] See Anderson, II. 177, 178. Some of the ministers of religion to whom the people of this new settlement looked for guidance taught them to regard the natives of the country as 'Canaanites,' the lawful objects of conquest and spoliation.

[3] It was Eliot who, at the end of a Grammar of the Indian language, wrote the memorable words, "Prayer and pains, through faith in Christ Jesus, will do anything."

which no kingly rule or ecclesiastical system might fetter, should regard without pity the ignorant savages around them, and think it better to burn and slay them as Amalekites, than to send among them the messengers of the Gospel of peace. "*O that you had converted some, before you killed any,*" is the pathetic remonstrance which the colonists of New Plymouth received from their former pastor at Leyden, when he had heard of their acts of hostility toward the Indians[1]. Well might the Sachems[2] complain that usurpation of their territories[3] and destruction of their villages afforded no encouragement to them to adopt the creed of these so-called Christians; and as they sullenly retired to the fastnesses of the forest or the wilds of the prairie, the barbarity of the savage heathen would have received fresh stimulus and intensity from the barbarity of the civilized Christian. Impressed, at first, with the superior power and wisdom of the white man, the Indians had imagined that the Great Spirit must have made these men of "finer dust" than themselves[4], but too soon they discovered that this superior race was tyrannical, and selfish, and cruel.

[1] Anderson, II. 195.

[2] "The principal chiefs were called Sachems, the subordinate ones Sagamores." *North American Missions* (R. T. S.), p. 6.

[3] The missionary Brainerd, when he first went among the Indians, was suspected of some ill design. "Two or three," he says, "were thus suspicious, and urged that the white people had abused them, and that therefore they had no reason to think that they were now concerned for their happiness, but, on the contrary, that they designed to make them slaves, &c."

[4] *From Pole to Pole*, p. 115.

The Moravian missions among the North American Indians, which were commenced in 1734, have on several occasions suffered from the cruel violence of white men. In 1782 a settlement of Christian Indians was entirely destroyed, and ninety-six persons cruelly murdered, thirty-four of the number being children[1]. And even so late as 1859 we hear of a murderous assault being made by Americans upon the mission of the Moravians at Westfield, the reason for it being, it would seem, nothing more than the wish to rid themselves of what they considered obstacles in the way of their possessing the country[2].

4. The cruelties of the Dutch farmers in South Africa, directed against the Hottentots and Bushmen, must next come under notice[3]. For a considerable period after the Dutch had settled at the Cape amicable intercourse existed between the colonists and the native Hottentots and other tribes. But as the number of colonists increased they began to encroach upon the land, and the Hottentots receded, and learned to look with suspicion and fear upon the intrusive settlers. Roving parties of "boors" (as the frontier farmers were called) surprised and plundered the kraals or villages

---

[1] For an account of this tragic occurrence, which, the writer says, "has scarcely a parallel in the annals of treachery and murder," see *North American Missions*, pp. 133—138.

[2] *From Pole to Pole*, p. 120.

[3] The opposition which these farmers raised to the *missionaries*, in the apprehension that they would no longer be enabled to serve themselves of the natives when they were educated, will be noticed in the next section (see below, p. 64).

of the inoffensive natives. A Dutch official who was sent into the interior of the country to procure some cattle for "the company," in the year 1705, was informed by some Hottentots, with whom he wished to transact business, that a certain free man by the name of drunken Gerrit, had, a few years before, come to their kraal with a party of men, "had fired upon them from all sides, burnt their huts, and carried off their cattle without their knowing any reason for it, since they had never offended any of the Dutch." They complained of other robberies, perpetrated by a neighbouring tribe, but "their most sorrowful and exasperated complaints" were about the wicked behaviour of this drunken Gerrit[1].

Marauding expeditions of this nature became common; and it was not long before the government became implicated in the oppression of the natives. This was in consequence of the representations made by the boors, who accused the natives of incessantly plundering the colonists. The fearful system of *Commandoes*, or military parties to exterminate the Bushmen, was instituted in 1754[2]. And, besides this authorized method

---

[1] Kupt's *Journal*, quoted in Philips' *South Africa*, Vol. I. p. 23.

[2] These commandoes "were usually raised by the different field-cornets, who collected the colonists on the frontier in their respective jurisdictions, having one commandant over the whole. They were to be armed, and to scour the neighbouring country to discover the abodes of the Bushmen; and when they espied a kraal they were to surprise it if possible, and, singling out the men, to shoot them. The surviving women and children were to be divided and shared among the members of the expedition or distributed among the neighbouring farmers." See Philips

of massacre, the boors killed the natives "as game or as noxious animals," whenever they came across them[1]. Hostilities never ceased for a day. The farmers considered it meritorious to murder a free Bushman, and spoke of shooting them "with as much composure and indifference" as if they were speaking of killing partridges. Barrow says that he heard one of "the humane colonists" boast of having destroyed with his own hand near three hundred of that unfortunate people[2]. The effect of this conduct on the part of the boors was, as might be anticipated, not favourable to the reputation of Europeans and Christians. They were regarded with horror and distrust by the natives around. The Hottentots had been found by the Dutch in a peaceful, independent, and prosperous condition. "In the course of about a century and a half they had been despoiled of their lands, robbed or cajoled out of their flocks or herds, and, with a few exceptions, reduced to personal servitude." "No attempts" (continues Mr Philips), "had been made to improve their moral condition, to restrain their passions or to refine their appetites....... As for religion, it was considered a crime to mention the subject to a native. They were not admitted within the walls of churches. By a notice stuck above the

(Vol. I. 42, 43), and a journal of Van Jaarsveld, quoted by him there. Compare Mr Thomson's account (Philips, Vol. II. 42). For some time the system was carried on under the *British* rule,—a fact which calls out the just indignation of the missionary. Vol. II. ch. ii. (See Appendix, Note H.)

[1] Philips, I. 53.   [2] Philips, I. 53.

doors of one of the churches, 'Hottentots and *dogs*' were forbidden to enter[1]."

The oppression and cruelty of the boors called out implacable enmity on the part of the natives who were free, or who succeeded in escaping from the servitude in which they had been held. The notable robber chief, Africaner, was goaded into becoming such by the cruelties of his Dutch employer. The Hottentots welcomed the Moravian and London missionaries when they came; but in proportion as the missionaries endeavoured to elevate and instruct the natives, did they for that very reason become objects of suspicion and dislike to the boors. For the object of the boors was "to keep the natives in a state of ignorance and slavery; and their love of uncontrolled authority ... shut their minds against every consideration which could be urged in favour of any attempt to improve them[2]." Is it wonderful that the Hottentots should rebel against tyranny like this? "We are blind heathens," said Klaas Sturman, a Hottentot chief, to some missionaries who were persuading him to lay down his arms and submit to the colonial government, "We are blind heathens, we know nothing, and in this state the boors wish to keep us; I wish to live a peaceable life, but I am determined to revenge the barbarous conduct of the boors to my people, till the government shall do us justice, and permit us to hear the Word of God[3]."

"Why is it," said a Bushman on another occasion

[1] Philips, I. 58.   [2] Philips, I. 86.   [3] Philips, I. 78.

(in an address delivered to his countrymen at a missionary station where some colonists were present) "that we are persecuted and oppressed by the Christians? Is it because we live in desert lands, clothe ourselves with skins, and feed on locusts and wild honey? Is there anything morally better in one kind of raiment, or in one kind of food, than another? *Was not John the Baptist a Bushman?* Did he not dwell in a wilderness? was he not clothed with a leathern girdle such as we wear? and did he not feed on locusts and wild honey? was he not a Bushman?... It is true John the Baptist was beheaded, but he was not beheaded because he was a Bushman, but because he was a faithful preacher; and where then do the Christian men find anything in the precepts or examples of their religion to justify them for robbing and shooting us because we are Bushmen[1]?"

The general effect of the cruel policy, and of the inhuman indifference to life, which the natives saw constantly exhibited before them by the white men on the frontiers of the colony was disastrous enough; for it aroused in the native mind feelings of anger and distrust; encouraged that "reciprocity of injuries[2]" which has so often characterised the establishment of

---

[1] Philips, II. 12, 13. For another remarkable testimony of one of these unfortunate people to the cruelty with which they were treated by the boors, see the deposition made by a Bushman chief named Uithaalder in the presence of Mr Philips and his companions (Philips, II. pp. 50—54). (Appendix, Note J.)

[2] See the account given of the outburst of Bushman animosity against the white colonists by a Hottentot. (Philips, II. 3 *note*.)

colonies in an uncivilized country; and delayed and impeded the progress of missionary efforts among the native tribes. Nor was the bad impression which was conveyed to the minds of the natives—and branded, we might say, into their memories by fire and sword—at all lessened by the conduct of travellers who penetrated into the interior of the country. "With the exception," says an excellent and well-known South African missionary, Mr R. Moffat[1], "of the solitary traveller whose object was of an entirely scientific character, those who ventured into the interior carried on a system of cupidity and perpetrated deeds calculated to make the worst impression upon the mind of the natives," who learned to regard Europeans "as an angry race of human beings only fit to be classed with the lions which roar for their prey in their native wilds. Intercourse with such visitors in the southern districts, and disgraceful acts of deceit and oppression committed by sailors from ships which visited Angra Piquem and other places on the western coast had... the most baneful influence on the native tribes, and nurtured in their heathen minds (naturally suspicious) a savage disgust for all intercourse with white men, alas! professedly Christian. Such was the long and deep-rooted impression made on their minds as a people that on one of the branches of the Fish-river...when I asked a native why he had never visited the missionary station, his reply was, 'I have been taught from my infancy to look upon hat-men (hat-wearers) as the

[1] *Missionary Labours and Scenes in Southern Africa*, Ch. v.

robbers and murderers of the Namaquas. Our friends and parents have been robbed of their cattle and shot by the hat-wearers.'"

Dr Livingstone also mentions the bad impression which was left by the violence and rapine of the boors who, calling themselves Christians, looked upon the coloured races as "black property." "They came," he says, "to the Bechuana tribes with the prestige of white men and deliverers" (i. e. from *native* oppression), "but the Bechuanas soon found, as they expressed it, that Mosilikatze," a native chieftain, "was cruel to his enemies, and kind to those he conquered, but the Boers destroyed their enemies and made slaves of their friends[1]." And when a native chief named Motebe was enjoined to live in peace, his reply was, "Teach the Boers to lay down their arms first[2]."

5. The treatment of Hottentots and Bushmen is in reality a collateral branch of the subject which next demands our attention, namely, the obstacles which have arisen to missionary success from *the Slave-trade* and *Slavery*. The history of the repartimiento system, and the cruelties consequent upon it in the Spanish and Portuguese possessions in South America, which has been already alluded to and partially illustrated in a previous section[3], is another branch of the same subject.

And indeed the history of the slave-trade in Africa has a very close connexion with the history of Spanish

---

[1] *Missionary Travels in South Africa*, Ch. II.
[2] *Ibid.* Ch. XXVI.   [3] See above, pp. 33—35.

conquests in America. The subjection of the Indians in the New World, and the introduction of negro slaves from Africa into the continent and islands of the West, are historically linked together[1]; and although the attempts at an Indian slave-trade in the Spanish possessions were put an end to by the measures of the Spanish government[2], the cruel and unjust servitude under which thousands of the aboriginal inhabitants of America perished differed little in its practical effect from that produced by the tyrannical system of oppression under which negroes have groaned, and toiled, and died; a system whose history "occupies one of the darkest pages in the records of this world[3]." The behaviour of the Spaniards and Portuguese towards the subject natives in their South American possessions must have often called forth the thought in reflecting minds, which the Jesuit historian of Paraguay has expressed: *Comment leur prêcher un Dieu bien de bonté qu'on les retenoit dans le plus dur esclavage*[4]?

There can be no doubt that the complicity of Europeans with the hateful traffic in men which has so long been carried on in Africa has proved a great impedi-

---

[1] See Helps, Vol. I. 220, 505; II. 21; IV. 370.
[2] Helps, Vol. IV. 376.
[3] Walker's *History of Church Missions in Western Africa*, p. 35.
[4] Charlevoix, *Histoire de La Paraguay*, Liv. v. One of the greatest hindrances to the Jesuit's missionary labours in Paraguay arose from "the Paulistas, or man-hunters of San Paulo," for an account of whom see Howitt's *Colonization and Christianity*, pp. 134 ff. And in Brazil the horrors of kidnapping, burnings of huts, fomenting of quarrels, formed a parallel to what we are accustomed to regard as peculiar to Africa and the slave traffic there. See Howitt, 154.

ment to the progress of the gospel in that continent. A quotation from the missionary Moffat's experience, given above, shews how the mind of the natives has been affected by the cruelties of modern settlers. And if we look back three or four hundred years, we shall see that from the time when Europeans first discovered the way to the West Coast, and round the Cape, there has been always ground for a deplorable connexion in the native mind between slavery and 'the white man[1].'

Wherever the Portuguese power extended the traffic in slaves was busily carried on; and Dr Livingstone, in giving a melancholy picture of a deserted missionary station where the Roman Catholic missionary once laboured, endeavouring, we may suppose, to teach something of the gentle and humanizing lessons of Christianity, attributes the failure of Portuguese missions to the participation of that nation in the slave-trade. This inhuman traffic, with all its painful accompaniments, was actually encouraged upon religious grounds. "The Portuguese missionaries in Africa, and the ecclesiastics at home, ceased not to represent to the civil powers the advantages conferred upon true religion by the transportation of the negroes from Africa .... to other countries[2]." Even the good Las Casas, whose beneficent labours for the Indians of the west were so remarkable,

---

[1] Moffat thought that a reference to slave-dealers might be traced in an answer made by a Namaqua to the missionary Schmelen, who asked, "How shall it be with you after death?" The answer was, "When we have died we go over the sea-water at that side *where the devil is.*"

[2] Walker, p. 37.

forgot himself, if we may so say, when he suggested that each Spanish resident in Hispaniola should have licence to import a dozen negro slaves. But he afterwards candidly acknowledged his error, and says that he gave this advice without considering the injustice of their capture by the Portuguese; "which advice, after he had apprehended the nature of the thing, he would not have given for all he had in the world. For he always held that they had been made slaves unjustly and tyrannically: for the same reason holds good of them as of the Indians[1]."

The traffic in slaves which has been kept up for so many years in Africa has been the means of fomenting and renewing wars in the interior, and so has maintained a barbarous state of things where legitimate and honest commerce might have done much to civilize and enlighten the rude and ignorant tribes; and has been the chief barrier to the prosecution of missionary enterprise in that country.

It was not only in Africa that slavery proved a hindrance to the progress and to the right appreciation of Christian truth. The 'Christian' slave-trader was one stumblingblock, the 'Christian' slave-owner became another. A "contemptuous indifference" with regard to the negro race grew up wherever they became subject to Europeans: and Christian nations recognized as a legitimate branch of trade " the slave business,—that violent outrage against the natural rights of mankind

---

[1] Helps, II. 18 (compare his repeated expression of regret, III. 216).

which is always in itself a crime, and leads to all manner of misdemeanours and wickedness[1]." Into, what has been rightly called, 'the sickening delineation' of the horrors of the slave-ship and the slave-market we need not enter here; nor is it necessary to expatiate upon the oppressive and barbarous acts by which many slaveholders have disgraced not only their profession of the Christian religion, but the very name of human beings[2]. It will be enough to give some evidence of the contemptuous disregard which was entertained among Christian people of the rightful claims to consideration on the part of the despised and ill-treated negro. Our instances shall be taken from the records of slavery as it existed in connexion with Christian and Protestant England.

The introduction of negro slavery into the North American colonies seems to have been due to a visit by a Dutch ship, which put in for purposes of trade at Jamestown in Virginia in the year 1620. Some of the settlers there purchased twenty negroes, which formed part of the ship's cargo. This purchase was speedily followed by others; and the slave-trade became a regular means of supply for labourers to work in the Plantations[3].

An Act of the Assembly of Maryland, in 1638,

[1] Sparrman, quoted by Philips, II. 13.

[2] For some account of the cruelties which have been "inflicted upon the hapless sons and daughters of Africa, by the Christian and civilized inhabitants of Europe," see Walker's *Church Missions in W. Africa*, pp. 42 ff.

[3] The import of slaves into the British Colonies from 1638—1786 is reckoned at 2,130,000. See Walker, p. 39.

avows the existence of slavery "in terms which imply that the poor slave was to be left, as a matter of course, without sympathy and without hope; as much a stranger to the blessings of Christianity, as he already was to those of temporal freedom." The Act " declares with a harsh brevity most significant of the utter indifference which was felt respecting them that the people consisted of all Christian inhabitants, 'slaves only excepted[1].'"

In the West Indies the English adventurers followed in the footsteps of "the Spaniards or roving pirates who preceded them; and regarded the slave as the *absolute property* of his master[2]." Ligon, in his *History of Barbadoes*, describes the manner in which the slaves were treated by the planters; and the following narrative will give a specimen of the cool inhumanity with which the masters neglected the highest welfare of their slaves. A negro had been ordered to attend on Ligon in some woods, through which pathways were being cut to a church, in process of erection there. This negro expressed astonishment and delight at a mariner's compass which Ligon had with him, and asked him several questions concerning it. After some while he asked to be made a Christian, thinking, Ligon writes, that "to be made a Christian was to be endued with all the knowledges he wanted." "I promised," he adds, "to do my best endeavour, and when I came home spake to the master of the plantation, and told him that poor Sambo desired much to be made a Christian. But his answer was that the people of that iland were governed

---

[1] Anderson, I. 489.   [2] Anderson, II. 94.

by the laws of England, and by those laws we could not make a Christian a slave. I told him that my request was far different from that, for I desired him to make a slave a Christian. His answer was, that it was true there was a great difference in that: but being once a Christian he could no more account him a slave; and by that means should open such a gap as all the planters in the iland would curse him. So I was struck mute, and poor Sambo kept quite out of church; as ingenious, as honest, and as good-natur'd poor soul as ever wore black or eat green[1]."

The planters contended that the negro "although he bore the resemblance of a man, had not the qualities of a man; a conceit, of which Godwyn boldly asserts, 'atheism and irreligion were the parents, and sloth and avarice the foster-nurses[2].'" They treated with severity any clergyman who sought to give religious instruction to the negroes; and the negroes themselves were dealt with more harshly and brutally than ever in consequence of the efforts on the part of some of the clergy to help them[3]. The negro was, in fact, in the eyes of West Indian planters, "a chattel, an instrument of husbandry, a machine to produce sugar, a beast of burden[4]," and not a responsible being, whose soul

---

[1] Ligon, quoted by Anderson, II. 65.

[2] Anderson, II. 298 (Godwyn was an Oxford man, a clergyman in Barbadoes. He published a pamphlet in 1680, entitled *The Negro's and Indian's Advocate*, &c.).

[3] See a case mentioned in Anderson, II. 301; and see below, pp. 67—69.

[4] Speech of Sir T. F. Buxton (*Memoir*, p. 116, 4th Edition).

demanded moral and intellectual culture,—a fellow-creature with faculties and feelings like those of his master.

The recommendations of the British government issued to the colonial authorities in 1823[1] sufficiently indicate the wretched state in which the slaves had been kept, and from which the noble band of 'abolitionists' were then striving to rescue them. Without religious instruction, without rights of property, without marriage, with no rights in a court of law, punished at the arbitrary will of their masters, their children taken from them, their women publicly whipped—this was the state of thousands of bondslaves who had Christian masters, but knew little of the Christian's God; who lived in a Christian land, but were left, for the most part, destitute of all Christian knowledge, and separated from all Christian sympathy.

Was there not in a state of things like this an accumulated and accumulating obstacle to the progress and acceptance of Christ's Gospel of peace and goodwill to mankind[2]?

6. The conduct of pirates and buccaneers[3] demands a brief notice in connexion with this part of our subject: for just as in the case of slave-traders in Africa, so here the violence and recklessness of these

---

[1] See Buxton's *Memoir*, pp. 117, 118.

[2] For a striking statement of the manner in which the wrongs of the slave touched the Christian conscience of men like Fowell Buxton, see his *Memoir*, p. 239.

[3] For the derivation of this name and origin of the organization of the body, see Cooley, II. 299.

European adventurers, who were the terrors of the seas, coasts, and islands wherever they came, must have left on the minds of the natives an impression by no means favourable to religion.

Let one instance suffice. Some piratical adventurers arrived at the Ladrone islands, immediately quarrelled with the natives, and killed a number of them. They went on shore every day, and fired upon the natives wherever they saw them. Some Indians were assembled peaceably on the shore. The treatment they met with at the hands of the European pirates—if that be a bad enough name—is described in "a vein of brutal jocularity" by one who accompanied the expedition. "Our people," he says, "that were in the boat let go in amongst the thickest of them, and killed a great many of their number. The others seeing their mates fall, ran away. Our other men who were on shore, meeting them, saluted them also by making holes in their hides[1]."

This contact with Europeans was not likely to prove beneficial to the morals of the poor heathen who survived the cruel attack upon them; and as they spake of the white men to each other they would probably be confirmed in the heathenish idea that the evil spirit is the deity to be worshipped, and fear of superior power the essence of religion.

[1] Cooley, II. 307.

Section II. Traders.

1. The selfish sensitiveness of Demetrius the Ephesian silversmith[1] is the type of a worldly minded cupidity which, alas! has not been confined to heathen image-makers. There have been Christians who preferred "the art whereby they got their wealth" to all considerations of Christian truth, and even of ordinary humanity.

Notably has this been the case in the dealings of Europeans with the aboriginal inhabitants of lands which they have conquered; but not only where they have subdued peoples, and acquired territories, has the commerce of Christian Europe hindered the advancement of Christianity. In China and Japan, for instance, where Europeans have never planted more than a precarious footing, the greed and rapacity of Christian merchants, their contests between themselves for filthy lucre's sake[2], their utter disregard of the principles not only of the Christian religion but of ordinary morality, have rendered the name of Christians odious, and put difficulties in the way of Christian missions which it will take years of persevering labour, on the part of those who have undertaken the good work, to overcome.

[1] Acts xix. 27.

[2] The natives of India saw "the Christian nations boasting themselves of their superior refinement and of their heavenly religion, fighting like furies, and intriguing like fiends one against another," in order to get the advantage in trading for sweet spices, silken robes, and precious stones. (See Howitt, pp. 190, 191.)

Portuguese, Dutch, English, all in turn have contributed to impress the nations of the East with the most unfavourable view of the character of Europeans. The eager pursuit of earthly gain, *argenti sitis importuna famesque*, has been the one great characteristic which has distinguished the operations of western nations in their intercourse with the peoples of the east, and "to this day," says a recent writer on China, "the character of Europeans is represented as a race of men intent alone on the gains of commercial traffic, and regardless altogether of the means of attainment[1]."

2. The story of European conquests and territorial acquisition reveals, as has been already in part shewn[2], a fearful amount of oppressive treatment by so-called Christians of those who came under their power. The reason of all this violence and cruelty was mostly a blind and selfish avarice. The lust of gold swept out of consideration the love of God, and with it, as was inevitable, the love of man also. Merchants multiplied who were eager to drive hard bargains with those

---

[1] Davis, *The Chinese*.

[2] Much more might have been said under the previous heading had it been necessary. The cruelties perpetrated by the Dutch in their Indian possessions were equal to all that the Portuguese had done before them: and the change from Roman Catholic to Protestant rulers was not for the benefit of the natives, who found that in perfidy and cruelty the latter equalled if they did not surpass the former. (See Howitt, p. 191.) The insolence and tyrannical conduct of the English in India might also have found place in the preceding section, but reference will be made to it in Section III. below. The French in North America vied with the English in their barbarous conduct towards the Indians. (See Howitt, pp. 315 ff.)

whose weakness exposed them to oppression, and whose ignorance exposed them to fraud. Missionaries were few and feeble in comparison with what they might and ought to have been, and their work was constantly opposed, and set at nought by men who "minded earthly things," and so were enemies to the cross of Christ.

The paragraphs which follow will be devoted to a few instances of the hostility with which efforts to Christianize the heathen have been met by such men as those just described.

3. The dealings of Europeans in North America shall supply us with our first example.

The views of a large proportion of English colonists are indicated in a remarkable sermon preached by William Crashawe before the first governor of Virginia. The preacher says that the reason why more did not come forward to "assist this present purpose of plantation" was, that the expedition did not give any hope of immediate profit. "Tell them," he says, "of getting XX. in the C. oh! how they bite at it; oh! how it stirres them! But tell them of planting a Church, of converting 10,000 souls to God, they are senselesse as stones; they stirre no more than if men spoke of toies and trifles: nay, they smile at the simplicitie, and laugh in their sleeves at the sillinesse of such as ingage themselves in these matters: but these men proclaime to the world what they bee, euen sows that still wallow in the mire of their present profit and pleasure, and being themselves unconuerted haue therefore no care to convert others. And indeed no marvell if having cast off all care of their owne salvation behind their backs they be insensible of others' miseries[1]."

The sale of ardent spirits was one of the chief grievances of which missionaries and converts complained. This fire-water, as the Indians called it, was pressed upon the natives by the white traders, who found the trade lucrative, and cared not for the obvious ill results which followed upon it. Not only did these Christian traders gain profit from selling rum, but by striking bargains with the Indians when these were intoxicated[2]: hence, their apprehensions, that should the sobriety and self-restraint of the Christian religion be attained by the Indians, all hope of their unlawful gain would be gone; and they endeavoured to frustrate the missionaries' exertions among the Indians both by open hostility, and by secret machinations[3]. The missionary Brainerd, in describing his experience, says that he felt, far more than the difficulties of his solitary way of living, the fear and concern that continually hung over his spirit lest the Indians should be prejudiced against

---

[1] Quoted by Anderson, I. 193.
[2] See Howitt, p. 394.
[3] *North American Missions*, p. 41. For a touching account of the evil done by the introduction of ardent spirits among the Indians, see the speech of a chief, named "White Turtle," to the Quakers at Baltimore in 1802, cited by Brown, *History of the Propagation of Christianity*, Vol. I., IV. § 6 (note). Comp. the words of a Canadian chief in a letter to Lord Goderich, quoted by Howitt, p. 381, and the remarks of Dr O'Meara in the *Conference on Missions* held in Liverpool, 1860 (p. 50). (Appendix, Note K.)

Christianity, and their minds embittered against himself, " by the insinuations of some who, although they are called Christians, seem to have no concern for Christ's kingdom, but would rather, (as their conduct plainly discovers) that the Indians should remain heathens, that they may with the more ease cheat and so enrich themselves by them."

4. The cruelty of the boors in South Africa has been already mentioned. We must now briefly notice their cupidity and avarice, and the consequent hindrances to the work and progress of missions in South Africa. They objected to the establishment of missions among the Hottentots on the plea that the natives would become wiser than themselves[1], and the interests of the colony would suffer. For some years missionaries were prohibited from labouring among the natives; and when the Moravians settled there, the boors kept up a pertinacious opposition to them. They "daily uttered the most abominable slanders against them; and had it been in their power it is probable that they would have murdered them outright. ... Besides they endeavoured to blast the labours of the missionaries by corrupting the people both in principle and practice. They attempted to make them disbelieve the word of God, and to despise the Saviour .... they laboured to seduce them to drunkenness, uncleanness and other vices[2]." When Dr Vanderkemp, one of the first mis-

---

[1] Brown, Ch. VI. § 10.
[2] Brown, Ch. IX. § 2. 1. Comp. Smith's *History of Missions*, Vol. I. p. 209, and II. 145.

sionaries of the London Missionary Society in South Africa, paid a visit to a Caffre chief named Geika, with the view of commencing missionary operations among the Caffres, a Dutchman named Priet Prinslo sent a message to the king, in which he accused the missionary and his companion of political designs, and represented them "as most dangerous persons, possessing poisoned wine, and sent into his country for the purposes of espionage and assassination[1]." When the same missionary, in conjunction with two others, gathered together some Hottentots for the purpose of instructing and educating them, at a place called Graaf Reinet, their labours were attended with a considerable degree of success. What was the consequence? Did the European Christians rejoice in the prospect of the elevation of their degraded fellow-creatures? On the contrary, their discontent was so great that they rose up in armed rebellion against the government, because the slaves and Hottentots were allowed to attend school and church! They complained that Hottentots and Caffres were 'put on a level with Christians' by being taught to read and write; and they demanded from the Commissioner of the district that the natives should be excluded from the church, "which should be purified, by having the seats washed, and the pavement

---

[1] Smith, II. 135. When Vanderkemp visited the Caffres on another occasion, the boors represented his journey as intended to stir up the Caffres against the colonists; and on his return to Graaf Reinet, he was shot at by the boors, who had taken possession of some of the houses there. (Philips, I. 70.)

broken up[1]!" When a missionary institution (in accordance with the express desire of the then governor, General Dundas) was formed for the Hottentots by Vanderkemp, it was viewed with feelings of hatred and jealousy by the boors, who did not hesitate to accuse the missionaries of being in connexion with the predatory Hottentots, and of causing their institution to be an asylum for robbers and murderers[2]. One of the greatest objections which the boors made to the English government under General Dundas was, the favour shown towards the natives, and to the efforts of the missionaries in their behalf: and when, by the treaty of Amiens, in 1802, the Cape of Good Hope was restored to the Dutch, the boors expected that the mission under Vanderkemp would be suppressed. Their reiterated misrepresentations so far prevailed upon Governor Janssens, that in April, 1805, the venerable missionary and his colleague Mr Read received an order to proceed to Cape Town without delay, to answer the charges preferred against them. Here they were detained, in suspense and inaction, for nine months, and were only prevented from putting into practice the resolve to which they had come to leave the country by the capture of Cape Town by the British in 1806.

Such was the hostility manifested to missionary

[1] Philips, I. 69. Smith (II. 140), adds another demand on the part of the boors, namely, "that the pulpit should be covered with black cloth, in token of mourning for the want of a regular clergyman" (!).
[2] Smith II. 143. (Comp. Vanderkemp's own words, Philips, I. 81.)

OBSTACLES TO MISSIONARY SUCCESS.

efforts among the Hottentots and Bushmen by those who called themselves Christians, and belonged to a people who professed to be zealous Protestants and stanch supporters of truth and liberty.

5. The most flagrant instance, perhaps, of the recorded hindrances to missionary work caused by the cupidity and covetousness of professed Christians, is to be found in the history of the planters and slave-owners in the British West Indies[1]. 'For more than one hundred years,' says Mr Philippo[2], a missionary in Jamaica, 'after Jamaica became an appendage of the British Crown scarcely an effort was made to christianize the negro slaves.' Nor was anything worth speaking of attempted for the religious conversion of the negro population of any of the islands under British dominion from the year 1624 to the year 1754. And when missions were set on foot in Jamaica and other islands, the planters and a great part of the white population manifested an incessant hostility to the missionaries. The intolerance, injustice, and cruelty, displayed in the persecution of the missionaries were fearful. Acts and ordinances were passed against 'irregular assemblies' and 'unlicensed preachers,' the restrictions of which amounted almost to a total prohibition of the slaves being religiously instructed by persons willing and com-

---

[1] The Moravian missionaries in the Danish colony of St Thomas experienced the same sort of opposition from the planters there as did the Wesleyans and Baptists in the English colonies. (See *From Pole to Pole*, p. 143.)

[2] *Missionary Guide Book*, p. 370.

petent to undertake that work[1]. Meetings for divine worship were interrupted; chapels were destroyed; missionaries were imprisoned; slaves who were guilty of the high crime of praying to God were ordered to be beaten and whipped: "the negro women who would no longer submit to the criminal desires of their masters" became the special objects of brutal tyranny; and all this was done by persons who professed much respect for the Church of England, and endeavoured to excuse their violence and intolerance by alleging that religion would not do for the slave population, it would make them seditious, it would cause a rebellion, and so forth; whereas, if only there had been more Christian instruction given to the poor blacks there would have been certainly less of that bitter feeling towards the white population which has more than once shown itself in the West Indies.

One of the most moving elements of the agitation in England for the extinction of slavery was the testimony which missionaries, banished from the islands, gave to the unjustifiable and unchristian measures which the planters took to put down the work of christianizing the unfortunate negroes. These Christian men, eager upholders of law and order, destroyed seventeen chapels, and inflicted upon the pastors and their flocks every species of cruelty and insult. 'I stake my character,' said Mr Buxton, 'on the accuracy of the

---

[1] See Duncan's *Narrative of the Wesleyan Mission to Jamaica* (Ch. III. and IV.). *From Pole to Pole*, pp. 145 ff. Brown, VII. § I. 8. Smith, II. 593.

fact that negroes have been scourged to the very borders of the grave, uncharged with any crime save that of worshipping God.' He adds, in reference to the unfortunate missionaries, 'There have not been in our day such persecutions as these brave and good men have been constrained to endure. Hereafter we must make selections among our missionaries. Is there a man whose timid or tender spirit is unequal to the storm of persecution? Send him to the savage, expose him to the cannibal, save his life by directing his steps to the rude haunts of the barbarian. But if there is a man of stiffer, sterner nature, a man willing to encounter obloquy, torture, and death, let him be reserved for the tender mercies of our Christian brethren and fellow-countrymen, the planters of Jamaica[1].'

Of the effect which the treatment that the missionaries received, and the refusal of the masters to allow their slaves to be taught to worship God, produced upon the negroes' mind, the following scene will enable us to judge. "The negroes crowded round the chapels where the persons of free condition might enter, but the door of which the poor slaves were forbidden to enter. Some might be heard exclaiming, 'Massa, me no go to heaven now:' 'White men keep black men from serving God:' 'Black man got no soul:' 'Nobody teach black man now.' The missionaries beheld them and wept, but durst say nothing[2]."

6. One more, and that a very notable instance of

---

[1] Buxton's *Memoir*, p. 248.   [2] Brown, VII. § 1. 8.

the opposition of 'the trading interest' among Christians to the work of missions among the heathen must not pass without notice here.

When the question of propagating Christianity in India became a matter of public interest in England, there arose what has been described as "a contest between the friends of Christianity and the advocates of heathenism[1]." The arguments used by the latter were to the effect that the introduction of Christianity into India would endanger our commercial interests and possessions in the East; and attempts were made to represent Hinduism and the Hindus as being a system and a people worthy of emulation in Europe[2].

It would perhaps be hardly accurate to say that the natives of India were directly affected by the progress of this controversy, either for good or for evil, at the time, but there can be little doubt that the hostile policy of the Indian Government,—as manifested in its treatment of the Baptist missionaries at Serampore, and of the American missionaries who were refused permission to stay in Bengal in 1812,—reflected the unreasonable apprehensions and unchristian selfishness of the party above alluded to,—and must have impressed the native mind with the fatal notion that a Christian government was not only utterly indifferent, but even opposed to the promulgation of Christian truth in the country.

[1] Foster, quoted by Kaye, p. 159.   [2] Hough, IV. 179.

Section III. Settlers.

1. We now come to the third division of our subject, and deplorable as the picture has already been, the darkest and dismallest shadows have yet to be put in. The cruel conqueror and the avaricious trader, in their treatment of others, have proved serious hindrances to the propagation of Christian truth in heathen countries: but nothing has been so prejudicial to the success of Christian missions as the immoral and irreligious conduct exhibited among Christians themselves in the sight of the heathen amongst whom they have sojourned or settled. Instead of gentleness, pride and insolence; instead of honesty, fraud and rapine; instead of purity and self-restraint, the most abandoned and reckless licentiousness; instead of godliness, impiety and infidelity: such is the sad description which those who have studied the history of the intercourse between European and heathen nations must often give of *Christians*, who, 'having a name to live,' have been, in truth, dead; dead to all the lofty aspirations, noble hopes, and high morality, which should characterize the followers of Him who "went about doing good," and who sent His disciples into the world with the special and significant charge to go and teach all nations, baptizing them into the sacred Name of the Triune God,—Father, Son, and Holy Spirit.

It will be at once seen that the subjects of the preceding sections belong also to this. The example, as well as the actual deeds, of the oppressor or the unjust and rapacious merchant became a hindrance to any attempts that were, or might be, made to induce the heathen to leave their own religion for the religion of Christians.

2. There was never perhaps a time when the responsibility of Christians to the heathen was entirely lost sight of in the schemes, political and commercial, which have stirred the hopes and elicited the activity of Europeans since the 15th century. The mistaken, but sincere and not ignoble, ambition of sovereigns like Isabella of Spain, or of leaders like Columbus and Cortez; the large hopes and lofty aims of men like Hariot and Hakluyt; the views expressed in the royal patents and charters given by James I. and Elizabeth, and in the narratives of Hales and Peckham; the personal piety of men like De La Warr, the first governor of Virginia, or Streynsham Master, governor of Madras[1]; are all cheering indications that both in public policy and private enterprise, the leaven of Christianity was still working even when the lump seemed almost entirely unleavened.

But if we take the whole history of the intercourse which has been opened up between Christian nations and the heathen in various parts of the world, we shall find that there is much more cause for shame than for glorying; and that so far from "providing things honest in the sight of all men," and being "as luminaries, holding forth the word of life," the conduct of

[1] See Anderson, I. 50, 68, 70, 159, 190; II. 277.

the majority of professed Christians has been rather that described by Ezekiel as the conduct of the Jews of old; *And when they came to the heathen whither they went, they profaned my holy name, since it was said of them, Jehovah's people are these, and from His land have they come forth*[1]. What wonder then that missionaries should be few and feeble; and the progress of their work tardy and limited? Even now when mission stations are multiplied, and much more zeal and interest in the propagation of the Gospel have been manifested than in preceding centuries, the words of Bishop Lake, in a sermon which he preached before Charles I. and the House of Lords, "On a Fast-day, July 2, 1625," are applicable still. After having said that it is not enough to make much of the possession of Christian truth for our own good, but that we should also endeavour to extend it to others, "Let me tell you," he proceeds, "that there lieth a great guilt upon Christian states[2], and this amongst the rest that they have not been carefulle to bring them that sit in darknesse and the shadow of death to the knowledge of Christ and participation of the Gospel. Much travelling to the Indies, East and West, but wherefore? Some go to possess themselves of the land of the infidel, but most by commerce, if by commerce, to grow richer by their goods. But where is the prince or state that

---

[1] Ezek. xxxvi. 20.

[2] We would rather say now 'Churches:' but it is an ill thing that secularization of political administration should proceed so far as to sever the vital union which should exist between the civil government and ecclesiastical organization of a Christian people.

pitieth their souls, and without any worldly respect endeavours the gaining of them unto God? Some show we make, but it is but a poore one; for it is but πάρεργον, an accessorie to our worldly desire; ἔργον it is not, it is not our primarie intention. Whereas Christ's method is Matt. vi. 33, 'First seeke ye the kingdom of God and then all other things shall be added unto you.' You shall fare the better for it in your worldly estate. If the Apostles and Apostolicke men had affected our salvation no more we might have continued till this day such as sometimes we were, barbarous subjects of the prince of darknesse[1]."

3. We proceed now to add to the already black catalogue of crimes of which we have shown European nations to be guilty in their intercourse with the heathen, a still further and not less damning indictment. A collection of all the evidence which we might bring forward to prove our case would fill a bulky volume; a selection is only difficult because there is so much from which to choose. Europeans have made their appearance and left their mark in every quarter of the globe: but wherever they have been, their conduct has been such as to place a stumblingblock in the way of the heathen, and has sorely impeded the success of the efforts made to spread the knowledge of the Gospel of Christ. In America, in Africa, in Asia, in Australia and the islands of the Pacific Ocean, the same melancholy tale repeats itself of Christians settling among heathen, and showing to them the example of wicked

[1] Quoted in Anderson, II. 189.

and unholy lives, spreading what have been called 'the vices of civilization' instead of the virtues of Christianity. Missionaries have they been, but not of God's sending. Following their own devices and neglecting His law, they have done the devil's work in the world, and not Christ's. These are hard words. Let the evidence which follows show that they are not too severe.

4. *Europeans in America.*

We have already seen that the cruelty of the Spaniards and Portuguese was a great impediment to the success of missions among the Indians. To this cruelty was added the vilest profligacy and dissoluteness of life. Southey, in his *History of Brazil*[1], tells us that the Jesuits[2] had greater difficulties than any fear which the cannibalism or savageness of the Indians might have inspired in the ill conduct of their own countrymen. This was a mightier obstacle to overcome than any of the idolatrous customs of the natives. "During the half century that the colonization of Brazil had been left to chance, the colonists were almost without law and without religion...A system of concubinage was practised among them worse than the loose polygamy of the savages; the savage had as many women as consented to become his wives, the colonist as many as he could enslave. There is an ineffaceable stigma upon the Europeans in their intercourse with those whom they treat as inferior races. There is a perpetual contradiction between their lust

---

[1] Ch. VIII.   [2] They were sent out under Nobrega in 1549.

and their avarice. The planter will one day take a slave for his harlot and sell her the next as a being of some lower species, a beast of labour..." The priests encouraged the colonists in these abominable acts, and publicly taught that it was lawful to enslave the natives and use the women as concubines. The truth was that the larger proportion of the first settlers in Brazil were Portuguese convicts; and the evils of the transportation of criminals from the mother country to a colony began to manifest themselves thus early in the history of European colonization. These convicts were more likely to communicate evil than either to teach or to learn good. "Their intercourse with the savages produced nothing but mischief; each made the other worse; the cannibals acquired new means of destruction, and the Europeans new modes of barbarity[1]."

There was one spot in South America where the Jesuit missionaries succeeded for a while in their endeavours to civilize and educate the native Indians. That spot was Paraguay. But the success of these missionary efforts depended much upon the isolation in which the Jesuits for a long while managed to keep their Christian settlements, or 'Reductions[2],' as they were called. A royal mandate was obtained that no Spaniard should enter these settlements except when going to the bishop or superior[3]. And a letter from the

---

[1] Southey's *History of Brazil*, ch. I.

[2] For an account of these Reductions, see Howitt, pp. 130, 131. Compare Southey (cited by Helps), Vol. II. ch. 24.

[3] Howitt, p. 132.

Bishop of Buenos Ayres to the king of Spain, in 1721, mentions the necessity which existed for such a mandate. The bishop says[1] that the intercourse of Spaniards with the Indians would be fatal to the innocence of the converts (*une peste fatale à leur innocence*), and would introduce all sorts of corruption. A like testimony is given to the need for such restrictions by the traveller Ulloa[2], who says that they were approved by all sensible persons, as by intercourse with Europeans the native Christians would lose all their docility, innocence, and piety. After the banishment of the Jesuits in the middle of the 18th century, the Reductions were placed in the charge of lay-commissioners (commandataires) with priests from the different mendicant orders under them. The previous tranquillity and welfare of the settlements of native Christians soon departed. The commissioners cared nothing for the education or evangelization of the natives; and the priests were sometimes as bad. The poor natives were unable to reconcile the oppressiveness and evil conduct of the Spaniards with the words which were spoken to them about the sweetness and holiness of the Christian religion[3].

Joseph Acosta, who laboured as a missionary for

---

[1] Charlevoix, *Histoire de La Paraguay* ('Pieces Justificatives' in prefatory chapter).

[2] Quoted by Charlevoix, Liv. v.

[3] "Ces infidèles ne pouvoient concilier cette conduite, ni les mauvais exemples qu'ils avoient souvent devant leur yeux avec ce quel'on disoit de la douceur et de la saintété de l'Evangile." Charlevoix, Liv. III.

fifteen years in Peru and the West Indies, confesses that there was no greater obstruction to the conversion of the Indians than the evil example of the Christians' wicked conduct[1].

There was one possibility of South America being speedily christianized; and that was *si tous ceux qui avoient quelque pouvoir sur les habitans eussent concouru avec les Missionaires pour les faire goûter les maximes de l'Evangile*[2]. But the taste given was not generally a taste for Christianity.

We do not find the matter very much mended when we proceed northward in the same continent from the Papists of New Spain to the Protestants of New England. Wherever missionary attempts were made in North America the complaint is still that the Christians' hindrances are the worst with which the work has to contend. The venerable Eliot complained of this; and Brainerd more than once expresses his sore grief at the prejudices against Christianity with which the minds of the Indians were filled on account of the vicious lives and unchristian behaviour of those who were called Christians. On one occasion, when preaching to the Indians, he was asked why he desired the Indians to become Christians. "The white people," said the chief, "lie and drink and steal more than their

---

[1] "De procuranda Indorum salute." Quoted by Hough, III. 117. Compare the remarkable will of a Spanish "Capitan," quoted by Helps, III. 504, in which he acknowledges that the corruption of the Peruvian people is due to the bad example set by the Spaniards. (See Appendix, Note L.)   [2] Charlevoix.

red brethren. It was they who first taught my countrymen to drink; and they stole from one another to such a degree that their rulers were obliged to hang them... but the Indians were never hanged for stealing; yet should they become Christians, it is probable that they would be soon as bad as the white people. They were resolved therefore to live as their fathers had lived, and to go to the same places as their fathers when they died[1]."

Besides the individual examples of unholy living,—of cruelty and lust, of avarice and rapine,—which the Indians of North and South America have had presented continually before their eyes by European Christians from the day when Columbus built the fort La Navidad[2], in Hayti, unto this very century of so much vaunted light and civilization,—they have witnessed "a constant scene of war and contention between the European powers terming themselves Christian." A passage, written with reference to Brazil, may be applied to this conduct of Europeans, and to the consequent hindrances of missionary success, throughout the double continent. French, English, and Dutch, like the Spaniards and Portuguese, were cruel and rapacious, not only in their dealings with savages, but in their contentions with one another[3]. "Every description of rapine,

[1] *From Pole to Pole,* p. 117.
[2] So called because he entered the port on Christmas Day, 1492. Alas! what a fearful contradiction has the whole career of European conquest in America given to the message of peace and good will by which that Day should be known!
[3] The instigations of the worst passions of the Indians by the English

bloodshed, and treachery, which can disgrace nations pretending to any degree of civilization, was going on before the eyes of the astonished natives. What notions of Christianity must these Indians have had when these people called themselves Christians? They saw them assailing one another, fighting like madmen for what in reality belonged to none of them; burning towns, destroying plantations; massacring all natives or colonists that fell into their hands, or seizing them for slaves. They saw bishops contending with governors, priests contending with one another[1], they saw their beautiful country desolated from end to end, and everything which is sacred to heaven or honourable and valuable to men treated with contempt.

"What was it possible for them to believe of Christianity than that it was some devilish compact, which at once invested men with a terrible power, and with the will to wield it for the accomplishment of the widest ruin, and the profoundest misery[2]?"

But it may be said, 'These remarks apply to a period which is past: surely missionaries have not the same complaints now to make as they had in times

---

and French in their contests for supremacy in North America were a definite barrier to all endeavours to Christianize or civilize the nations. (See Howitt, p. 315.)

[1] This sentence is only applicable to the Roman Catholic nations in the south. But we read that in the Pequod war (of which mention has been already made in this essay) the English in their murderous assault upon the Indians were "animated by the exhortations and prayers of their ministers." (And see note, above, p. 43.)

[2] Howitt, p. 154.

gone by.' Two chapters in Mr Howitt's *Colonization and Christianity*[1] will suffice to undeceive persons who think that human nature in the nineteenth century is necessarily better than it was in the fifteenth. It appears that in spite of declarations and treaties in which the natural rights of the Indians were repeatedly recognised by the United States of America, the abominable and untrue doctrine that the Indian tribes, as "savage and irreclaimable," should be pushed away out of the path of "civilized" man, has not only been broached, and speculatively discussed, but maintained and relentlessly carried into practice; and that, moreover, when some of the Indian tribes were giving the lie to this monstrous doctrine by a fast advance in civilization, and by adopting orderly and settled habits, "conforming both to the religion and the habits of the Americans"—missionaries, and especially the Moravians, labouring amongst them with the most signal success—the Americans, instead of welcoming and helping forward the growth of "this young Indian civilization[2]," directed against these very Indians more strenuous efforts than ever to drive them out of their lands, and take possession themselves. And what is the language of the Indians who have not listened to the missionary, and have refused to become Chris-

---

[1] Ch. XXIV, XXV.

[2] A very interesting description of the progress of Christian education, and the consequent elevation of the people, among the Cherokee Indians, is to be found in Howitt, pp. 405—409. (See Appendix, Note M.)

tians? From the days of Eliot and Mahew and Brainerd it has always been the same. Sometimes plaintive, sometimes indignant—at one time referring with sorrow or anger to the unjust seizure of their territories by the white men, at another time with astonishment or scorn to the wicked and unprincipled lives of the Europeans—it has always been to the same effect. "See," they have said to the missionaries, "if your teaching be true, let us behold the results of it in your countrymen. Make them good and just and gentle. And then come and preach to us."

The vicinity of a white settlement has been always a formidable obstacle to missionary work. In Georgia, when a chief named Tomichichi "was urged to listen to the doctrines of Christianity, he keenly replied, 'Why these are Christians at Savannah! these are Christians at Frederica!' Nor was it without good apparent reason that the poor savage exclaimed, 'Christian much drunk! Christian beat men! Christian tell lies! Devil Christian! Me no Christian[1].'"

So the Moravians in Labrador found that the Esquimaux who had been brought most into contact with Europeans were the worst; and that when some of their converts visited the European settlement, they came back with a much more unfavourable idea of Christianity than when they went.

But we need not multiply testimonies. Sufficient has been said to indicate that the course of European

[1] Southey's *Life of Wesley*. Exactly similar language was held in India with reference to the conduct of Europeans there.

Christians for the three and a half centuries, during which they have gradually subdued, and occupied almost the whole of America, has not been such as to commend the name of Christians, or help forward the propagation of Christianity among the heathen.

Missionaries have been few, and mission work has been feeble; but the greatest obstacle of all to the success of the work has been "the defective moral and religious condition" of the European conqueror, trader, and settler with whom the aboriginal inhabitants have been brought into such mournful and baleful association.

5. *Europeans in Africa.*

Almost all that need be said in this essay with reference to the ill effects of the conduct of Europeans in Africa as affecting the progress and success of missions has been already brought forward[1].

A few more words may be added with reference, first, to the ancient Roman Catholic missions, and then to the enlarged prospects of modern missionary enterprise.

It appears that in the Portuguese missions, and especially in the Congo mission, dissensions arose between the Jesuits and other orders of monks. This discord, together with the fact that many of "the priests and monks to whom the care of religion was entrusted, became immersed in luxury and licentiousness, or in schemes of ambition inconsistent with their sacred character[2]," caused the mission work to drag

---

[1] Above, pp. 45—54.   [2] Walker, p. 151.

heavily. It seems also, from the slight vestiges which are left of the Portuguese missions, that the evil system of accommodation to the prejudices of the heathen had been employed in Africa as it was in India and China.

The whole course of Protestant missionary enterprise in Africa has been impeded, opposed, and in some places rendered impracticable, by the selfish and tyrannical conduct of Europeans. On the west coast the slave trade, in the south the unjust wars and cruel enslavement by which the aboriginal tribes were embittered against the white colonists, have been the chief reasons why Christianity has made so little progress in Africa. For a long while after the English came into possession of the Cape, the oppression of Hottentots, Bushmen, and Caffres was continued with the same reckless want of consideration and humanity as had characterised the period of the Dutch rule[1]. And the complaints of the natives were similar to those of the Red Indians in America. When a missionary addressed a Bechuana on the subject of religion, and seemed to have made some impression on him, the mournful question was asked, "Do the people *who killed my children and took away my cattle believe these things?*" 'Commandoes' for the purpose of exterminating hostile tribes were not a likely method of conciliating the minds of the savages, and commending the message which the missionary wished to give to them.

[1] See Philips' *South Africa* (passim); and Howitt, ch. xxvi. xxvii.

And in some cases the missionary work which had been already begun was stopped by the barbarism—for so it must be called—not of the savages, but of their Christian neighbours. "Whenever," said a Caffre chief who had had at his own place, before one of the wars had broken out, a missionary, and a church attended by 300 people,—"Whenever the missionaries attempt to preach to the Caffres, or whenever I myself preach or speak to my countrymen, they say, 'Why do not the missionaries first go and preach to the people on the other side? why do they not preach to their own countrymen, and convert them first'?" On one occasion a Caffre chief, who had dared to cross the colonial frontier, (after having been refused permission by a military officer), for the purpose of attending *a missionary meeting*, and who had been recommending the establishment of a mission among his own countrymen, was arrested "in the most brutal and insulting manner, and not without considerable hazard to the chieftain's life from the ruffian-like conduct of a drunken sergeant, although not the slightest resistance was attempted[2]."

But a new and more rational policy than that of commandoes and patrols has been adopted. And the travels of the energetic and kind-hearted Livingstone are, it is to be hoped, an omen of, and preparation for, the time when commerce will be conducted on Christian and humane principles, and the conquests of the sword be superseded by the bloodless victories of the Christian missionary. The labours of the London Society Mis-

---

[1] Howitt, p. 468.   [2] Howitt, p. 456.

sionaries and of the Moravian brethren have vindicated the character of black men from the unreasonable aspersions of interested oppressors, and have proved that the Bushman, the Hottentot, the Caffre, and other tribes of savages, are capable of Christian instruction, and can be raised by Christian civilization to an intellectual, social, and moral position, which can elicit the admirarion and respect of the citizen, and the thankfulness of the Christian[1].

6. *Europeans in Asia.*

The history of the European settlements in India in its reference to missionary work among the heathen contains more to sadden the Christian's heart than any other history in the world. What has been left undone in the way of help, what has been done in the way of hindrance, can hardly be calculated. When the Portuguese landed at Calicut, in the year 1497, they found existing on the south-west coast of India Christian churches which knew nothing indeed of the Pope and of Rome, but were certainly not without claims upon the sympathy and help of their brother Christians. These Churches of Syrian Christians the Portuguese persecuted, and almost crushed, with the weight of papal tyranny and intolerance which they used against them. When the Dutch and English came, oppression was followed by contempt or indifference: and the Christians of Malabar were regarded, or disregarded, to the same extent as the heathen around them. But

---

[1] See this exemplified in the history of the Griquas, Philips, II. 56.

the worst feature of the history of the European settlements in India is the unchristian character of the settlers; and nothing has been such an obstacle to the conversion of natives as the unholy lives of the professed Christians with whom they came into intercourse.

A few out of many testimonies must be brought forward in substantiation of this statement.

Maffeus[1] says, speaking of the Portuguese, that there was no greater hindrance to the spread of Christianity than the spectacle of Christians living a life of utter contradiction to the religion which they professed; and confesses that the virtuous life of the few was of far less influence than the vicious life of the majority, *neque enim tantam spectata paucorum innocentia et virtus adstruit Evangelis fidem, quantam insignis multorum et notissimi fere cujusque avaritia et improbitas adimit.*

The Abbé Raynal[2] gives a deplorable picture of the general demoralization of the Portuguese in India, and corroborates the statement just quoted from Maffeus. What likelihood was there of success in missionary work, when those who called themselves Christians "made no scruple of pillaging, cheating, and enslaving" the natives, sometimes with, and oftener without, a religious pretext: and when their manners were such as the historian describes by calling them "a mixture of avarice, debauchery, cruelty, and devotion. They had most of them," continues Raynal, "seven or eight

---

[1] Quoted by Kaye, p. 16.
[2] Quoted by Howitt, pp. 178 ff.

concubines, whom they kept to work with the utmost rigour, and forced from them the money they gained by their labour....The chiefs and principal officers admitted to their tables a multitude of those singing and dancing women with which India abounds."

Was it surprising that under the regime of Christians like these men the progress of Christianity should be slow[1]?

The faulty system of missionary work used by the Dutch in Ceylon has been before mentioned as affording no inconsiderable obstacle to the progress of true Christianity among the natives. It must be remembered that the prevailing hypocrisy among the native Christians (as they called themselves), which was in a great measure due to this system, was also fostered by the evil example of the Europeans themselves. And when in 1730 the Dutch consistory in Galle put on record their views of the obstacles which prevented the growth of Christianity, they blamed especially "the licentious and offensive lives of the Europeans who encourage the natives in debauchery and show them an example in the practice of every vice[2]."

The Protestant mission which laid the foundation of the missionary work which has been since carried

---

[1] A little before Xavier came to Goa, the king of Portugal "sent out an ecclesiastic to ascertain the cause of the slow progress of Christianity in India." Hough, I. 175. (For a further testimony to the bad character of the Portuguese in India, see Sepulveda, quoted by Steinmetz, Book v.)

[2] Palm's account of the Dutch Church in Ceylon, quoted by Tennent, p. 57.

on by English and Americans in India, was the Danish mission at Tranquebar. And we find that one of the chief impediments to the success of the missionaries was the fearfully immoral and irreligious condition of the Europeans[1]. "All our demonstrations," say the earliest missionaries, "about the excellency of the Christian constitution make but a very slight impression while they find Christians generally so much debauched in their manners, and so given up to gluttony, drunkenness, lewdness, cursing, swearing, cheating and cozening, notwithstanding all their specious pretences to the best religion. But more particularly are they offended with that proud and insulting temper which is so obvious in the conduct of our Christians here[2]." Similar testimony is afforded again and again in the life of the eminent missionary Swartz.

A Hindu merchant once said to him, "Sir, be not displeased, I wish to ask you a question. Do all Europeans speak like you?" When Swartz replied, that all Europeans were not truly Christians, but those who were so prayed that the Hindus might come to the knowledge of Christ, "You astonish me," said the merchant, "for from what we daily observe and experience

---

[1] It must not be forgotten that besides the actually existent and apparent immorality of the Europeans at the time, the missionaries had to contend against the unfavourable impressions which had been spread throughout India for the two previous centuries concerning the irreligious conduct of the Feringhis. An appalling account of the immorality of the early English settlers in India is given by Kaye, ch. II. Compare Terry's *Voyage to East India*. See Appendix, Note N.

[2] Hough, III. 119.

we cannot but think Europeans with but few exceptions to be self-interested, incontinent, proud, full of illiberal contempt and prejudice against us Hindus and even against their own religion, especially the higher classes. So at least I have found it with the majority of those with whom I have had any intercourse[1]."

On another occasion one of the unfortunate class of dancing girls, in reply to a remark made by the missionary that no unholy person should enter the kingdom of heaven, said, "Ah! sir, in that case hardly any European will ever enter it."

Dubois' *Letters on the State of Christianity in India*, published in 1823, abound in statements of the evil influence exercised upon the natives by the irreligious lives of professed Christians. He tells us that he was often seriously asked by them whether the Frangy[2] acknowledged and worshipped a God; and that "it is a well-known fact that it is precisely those of the Hindoos who are most familiar and most connected with the Europeans who manifest the strongest disgust and aversion to the religion and manners of the latter[3]."

The general impression of the natives has been in accordance with what a Musalmán said on having a Persian New Testament given to him, "It is very good," he remarked, "but the Sáhib Lóg[4] do not live accord-

---

[1] Pearson's *Life of C. F. Swartz*, ch. II.
[2] Or Feringhi, i.e. Europeans.
[3] Dubois, p. 48.
[4] 'The Gentlemen,' i.e. Europeans.

ing to their book. I have only seen one or two that do so."

A vast improvement, indeed, in the moral and religious aspect of European society has taken place of late years in India. But until recently the whole weight of European influence was antagonistic to Christian Missions[1].

When Kiernander came to Bengal, and commenced missionary work in Calcutta, he met with "little sympathy and less encouragement" from the Christian community. Indeed it was hardly a Christian community in any thing but name. "Men drank hard and gamed high, concubinage with the women of the country was the rule rather than the exception. It was no uncommon thing for English gentlemen to keep populous zenanas[2]." Duelling was considered creditable; acts of shameless lust were looked upon as not only harmless but laudable. "What in those days was the representation given of our holy religion to the natives of India? It was held up to their view as a religion of revenge, of avarice, of malice; as a religion that encouraged every evil passion, every wicked word, and every ungodly work.... When the missionaries went among the heathen to propagate the Gospel, what was the reply they met

---

[1] The indifference manifested to Christianity, and the indulgence afforded to heathenism by the policy of government, has been decidedly unfavourable to the reputation of the Christian religion in the eyes of the natives. The whole subject is too difficult and delicate a one to be dealt with in the paragraph of an Essay. See Appendix, Note O.

[2] Kaye, p. 95.

with? 'Why do you come amongst us? why not teach and reform your own countrymen? What! would you have us to adopt such a religion as yours? to abandon the system of our ancestors, to become drunkards and swearers and blasphemers and adulterers? You tell us that if we remain heathen we shall perish. Better that we should thus suffer than adopt a religion like this[1].'"

Since that time the tone of Christian society has become at least decorous and respectable where it cannot be called religious. But even now the reports of missionaries and the testimony of others bear witness to the hindrances which are not seldom put in the way of missionary success in India by the conduct of professed Christians there[2].

7. *Europeans in Australasia and New Zealand.*

The efforts to carry on missionary work in Australia have failed; in New Zealand they have in some measure succeeded; in the South Sea Islands a large measure of success has resulted. But the chief hindrances in all cases have arisen and are arising from the unchristian conduct of settlers or voyagers.

In Australia the evil effects of the transportation[3]

---

[1] *British India*, by Rev. W. Campbell, a missionary.

[2] See Rev. R. C. King's remarks at Missionary Conference in Liverpool, and the late Bishop Cotton's article on the Tinnevelly missions, the success of which missions is in some degree attributed to their being further removed than other places from close intercourse with Europeans. Appendix, Note P.

[3] For some remarks on this subject, see *Church Missionary Intelligencer*, Oct. 1858. Arnold, quoted by Anderson, II. 75. Howitt, p. 470.

system soon showed themselves. A parliamentary Report in 1837 states that in the plantation of the penal settlements "the territorial rights of the natives were never considered, and very little care has since been taken to protect them from the violence or contamination of the dregs of our countrymen." Incessant acts of mutual hostility between the natives and the colonists (who were at first composed of liberated convicts) generated a spirit of hatred and revenge on both sides; but the first fault lay with the rapacity and violence of the white settlers. The more the natives came in contact with the Europeans, the worse did their condition become, and now in spite of some efforts to educate and Christianize them they have become extinct[1].

The history of the intercourse between Europeans and the inhabitants of New Zealand previous to the colonization of that island shows that the savages were often less barbarous than the traders and sailors who called themselves civilized. And there can be no doubt that this intercourse encouraged and excited the worst natural passions of those who might have been softened and refined by Christian teaching and example[2].

[1] See Bp. Broughton's *Charge* quoted in Howitt, p. 476.
[2] See for instances of cruelty and recklessness on the part of masters of trading vessels and others, Thomson's *Story of New Zealand*, Part II. c. ii. Whalers, sealers, and runaway convicts who sometimes naturalized themselves in New Zealand and became what were called "Pakeha Mauris," behaved in a manner calculated to strengthen heathenism rather than to prepare the way for Christianity. Comp. Ellis, in *Polynesian Researches*, c. II. and Howitt, pp. 486 ff. See Appendix, Note Q.

When the island was colonized the great obstacle which was raised to missionary work arose from the aggressive conduct of the settlers, who looked upon the natives as being the sole barrier to their possession of the land, and used most unjustifiable means[1] for procuring territory for themselves by taking advantage of the ignorance and simplicity of the natives; and then met the discontent, which arose when the natives found that they were cheated, by waging wars which were as unjust as the commandoes in South Africa, already mentioned.

The records of the missions to the South Sea Islands, commenced in 1797, form one of the most interesting portion of missionary annals; and afford the plainest proof that "Christianity prepares the way for, and necessarily leads to, the civilization of those by whom it is adopted[2]." But we may not dwell here on the fair parts of the picture which might be presented to us. It is our melancholy task to shew the great danger by which these promising missions are threatened. Before the missionaries came, the islanders had had frequent and bitter experience of the ill conduct of white men in the shipping which every now and then touched at their shores. The writer of *Polynesian Researches*[3] makes the following statement. "It is a

---

[1] See especially the system of '*land sharking*' as described by Thomson.

[2] For a short account of the transformation which the native habits of the Tahitian and Society Islands have undergone in consequence of the introduction of Christianity, see Howitt, pp. 479—483.

[3] C. IV.

melancholy fact that the influence of unprincipled and profligate foreigners has been more fatal to the missionaries, more demoralizing to the natives, more inimical to the introduction of Christianity, and more opposed to its establishment, than all the prejudices of the people in favour of idolatry, and all the attachment of the priests to the interests of their gods." When ships came to the islands where missionaries resided, they were always glad when none of the sailors were left on shore, for they had often occasion to observe "the baleful influence of unprincipled seamen upon the minds and habits of the natives[1]." On one occasion Mr Williams met two sailors who went about baptizing the natives, and pretending to heal the sick by saying "a bit of a prayer over them" for the purposes of extorting money: and he speaks of the number of runaway sailors and convicts, whose residence among the inhabitants of the Navigation islands did them incalculable mischief. This is the class of men to whom Howitt alludes[2], when he says that "a roving class of sailors and runaway convicts have revived once more the crimes and character of the old bucaniers. They go from island to island diffusing gin, debauchery, loathsome diseases, murder, as freely as if they were the greatest blessings Europe had to bestow. They are the restless and triumphant apostles of misery and destruction; and such are their achievements that it is declared that unless our government interpose some

---

[1] Compare Williams' *Missionary Enterprises*, ch. XXVII.
[2] P. 485.

check to their progress, they will as completely annihilate the islanders as the Charibs were annihilated in the West Indies[1]." The enormities perpetrated in New Zealand and the islands of the Pacific by men like these, equal, if they do not surpass,—and perhaps, when we consider the period of the world's history, they do in moral guiltiness surpass—the most fearful atrocities committed by the Spaniards three centuries ago. One comforting reflection there is that now these actions are not looked upon as chivalrous, and they are performed by the lowest and vilest class of Europeans. The impediment which they present to missionary success is obvious.

We must close this chapter of sad and melancholy history. Its contents have been necessarily somewhat fragmentary and disjointed. A few concluding words, in which the substance of what has been said may be gathered up, and be connected with the more general aspect of the missionary subject, are yet required.

[1] For proofs of this statement, Howitt mentions at the place above quoted the testimonies of Messrs. Ellis and Williams to various lawless and murderous acts perpetrated by crews of vessels and runaway sailors in New Zealand and the Society Islands.

CHAPTER III.

RECAPITULATION, AND CONCLUDING REMARKS.

FROM the facts presented in the preceding chapter there can be no doubt that the candid inquirer into the history of missionary efforts amongst the heathen will acknowledge that those efforts have met with—one might almost say, *infinitely*—more of hindrance than of help from the great body of professing Christians. And so far from being disappointed with the amount of success already obtained he will rather be surprised that so much has been done where the difficulties and discouragements have been so many and so great. The propagation of Christianity in the world has been slow and limited, not because of any insufficiency in the doctrines which it promulgates or uncertainty in the facts upon which those doctrines are based, but because men have contented themselves too often with an external and heartless adoption of the doctrines, and an utter forgetfulness of the significance of the facts of Christianity. They have thought too much of the profession of the Christian religion, and too little of union with Christ; too much of forms and observances, and too little of truths and principles; too much of political expediency, and too little of moral rectitude; too much of the seen and temporal, and too little of the unseen and eternal. The one word which denotes at once the corruption of Christianity and the essence of heathenism is *worldliness*. This it is which has so often degraded the professed Christian and prevented him from fulfilling his high mission in the earth. He has never risen to the spiritual and heavenly standing-point of his Divine Master. He has been, to use the striking language of Scripture, "of the earth, earthy." Outwardly a Christian, he has been in reality a man of this world; selfish, carnal, godless; ignorant of, and careless about, the higher and nobler spiritual life which Christ gives to those who receive Him.

We have seen in the historical review which we have been taking of the dealings of Christians with heathen ample proof of the above statement, and much more might have been added. Cruelty, avarice, indifference to religious truth and therefore to morality, have all been exemplified. We have seen also that methods have been used to propagate the Christian religion which have been in defiance of the fundamental principles for the development of which Christ came down from heaven, to wit, mercy and justice and truth.

The heathen have, in many instances, been destroyed in their heathenism by the cruelty of Christians, left in their heathenism by the neglect of Christians, confirmed in their heathenism by the evil example of Christians.

It has been said that 'Christianity cannot exist apart from civilization.' The more correct statement would be that civilization cannot exist apart from Christianity.

Christianity cannot, indeed, exist *apart from* civilization, for the simple reason that it is itself a humanising and civilizing power. But civilization without Christianity is neither deep nor lasting. When, for instance, we consider the 'civilization' of ancient Egypt of China, of India, of Persia, in the East, or of Greece and Rome in the West, before the Christian era, we find a want of progressive vitality which indicates the absence of some essential element of national wellbeing. In the Eastern nations the civilization has been mainly external. The internal, germinant, moral power, without which neither a nation nor an individual can become truly great, was not developed. A huge giant, clothed in silk, and glittering with barbaric pomp of gold and jewels, with much of physical might but little of mental energy, and less of moral discernment, is not an unfit emblem of the most famous empires of the East. And when we turn to the two Western nations, whose history, after that of the Jewish people, holds the most important part in the development of the human race, we find that the *intellectual* element of civilization, represented by Greece, was restless, speculative, oligarchic; while the *political* element, represented by Rome, was ambitious, centralizing, tyrannical. There was neither the stability of principles, nor the liberty of persons, which our modern civilization has, and which, so far as it possesses them, it entirely owes to the spread of Christianity. Nor was the mass of society penetrated by any high moral ideas or religious aspirations. There was place for the philosopher and the conqueror, but 'the common people' were little thought of, and little cared for[1].

At the best, then, the old civilization was aristocratic and limited, and there was no diffusive glow of life pervading the social system. But Christianity changed all this. While its message was for all, high and low, rich and poor, one with another, that message was only acceptable to those who acknowledged the need of a redemption from evil which human power and wisdom could not give. *To the poor* the glad tidings were given that GOD loved man; and the Divine *philanthropy*[2], as manifested in Christ Jesus, began that course of emancipation of the human mind from error, and of the lowest of the human race from oppression and bondage, which has been the peculiarly *Christian* element of modern civilization, and which is to issue one day in that universal service of God which will be the perfect liberty and happiness of all nations.

And the very fact that the beneficial results of Christianity were first felt at the bottom of the social scale, and that they worked upwards from below, is proof enough that, if we wish to elevate from barbarism,

---

[1] See Milman's *History of Christianity*, Vol. I. p. 33 (edition of 1867). Comp. Neander's *Church History*, Vol. I. p. 40, and *Memorials of Christian Life*, pp. 1. 11, 18, 19 (Bohn's editions).

[2] See Tit. iii. 4.

Christianity is the lever which we may most hopefully use. When we consider, moreover, that the two principal constituents of civilization are, as M. Guizot has pointed out, the progress of society and the development of the individual, where shall we find a greater promoter of civilization than in a religion which contains all that is most necessary, both to regulate and to stimulate human action; which establishes a bond of universal brotherhood, while it satisfies the religious cravings of each soul that accepts its mighty facts and pure doctrines; and unites men together in an identity of faith and hope, while it brings each individual conscience and heart into direct relation with the eternal love of God? Christianity is alike favourable to order and to liberty; and, in proportion as it is rightly apprehended in its relations to social and individual welfare, do men deliver themselves from anarchy on one side and tyranny on the other, while all that is calculated to further the intellectual and moral elevation both of individuals in their separate capacity and of communities in their corporate action is either contained in, or is assisted by, the revelation of God's love to man in Christ Jesus our Saviour. For, assuredly, the real progress of the world must depend upon the knowledge which men may acquire of their true relations to the Creator and Moral Governor of all; and the furthest unfolding of this knowledge is in the New Testament. Our modern progress, so far as that progress is *beneficent*, is owing to the influence of Christianity both in arousing and in directing the moral and emotional energies of human nature. In all the growth of art, in all the problems of politics, in all the issues raised by philosophy, in all the applications of physical science, there are continual points of contact with the moral and religious cravings and claims of the human mind and conscience[1]. And the religion of Christ, by making the satisfaction of these claims the paramount object of pursuit by the individual soul, exercises a moral control over the whole development of national, social, and domestic life.

If, then, we wish to raise human beings from a state of degradation, and to ameliorate their physical, intellectual, moral condition, we must ourselves act upon, and do our best to communicate, the blessed truths of the Christian religion.

The reason why so few savage tribes have been civilized is that they have not been fairly used by the people who came amongst them, calling themselves Christians. These so-called Christians for the most part despised, oppressed, cheated the savages, instead of endeavouring to reclaim them and teach them the revelation of God in Christ Jesus.

The instances of the Cherokees in North America, the Griquas in Africa, and the South Sea islanders in the Pacific (to all of whom allusions have been made in this essay), are clear and satisfactory proofs that the

[1] "How is it possible to attain to a just and correct knowledge of human things in any department of life and science, unless they be viewed in relation to and connexion with the divine principle which animates or directs them." Schlegel's *Philosophy of History*, p. 275 (Bohn's edition).

true way to civilize is to Christianize[1]; and that the words of Livingstone—which might well serve as a motto for our travellers and colonists as well as for our missionaries—are true words: *Christians have never yet dealt fairly by the heathen and been disappointed.*

Christians have often boasted themselves of a superior civilization, and have forgotten that the true source and preservative of civilization are to be looked for in the moral and religious truths of Christianity, rather than in the mercantile and political maxims of worldly wisdom. If only they had remembered this, and acted accordingly, how changed the world's history might have been!

Success then to all missionaries who are sowing among heathen people the good seed of the word of God. Let the worldly-minded taunt them, let the philosophers despise them; yet are they laying the only foundation on which human happiness, even in this world, can be built. It would be better to spend more money on our missionary societies, and we should have less to spend in our military and naval preparations abroad: better too to spend more money in Christian education at home, that so as our youth grow up and diffuse themselves over the world's surface they may prove helps and not hindrances to the great missionary cause. And this cause is, if we will but look at it closely enough, not a separate work from evangelization at home, but a branch of it, fed by the same sap, lively

---

[1] See also an interesting account of the Metlahkatlah settlement in North West America. *Church Missionary Intelligencer*, March, 1865.

when that is lively, dull and lifeless when that is weak and puny.

For, in the first place, the missionary's work abroad and the minister's work at home are essentially the same. The form, the conditions, and the phase of work may be different, yet the work itself is, both in one case and the other, to bring souls to Christ, and to build them up in the faith and love of God. And, secondly, the very diversity of circumstances which distinguishes these two portions of the one great work, which the Christian Church has to do *wherever* she has opportunities given her to do it, proves beneficial to both. The interest in missionary work among the heathen kindles a feeling of devotion to the cause of Christ and to the salvation of perishing souls, which by a kind of reflexive power invigorates and refreshes the interest felt in the promotion of Christian education and evangelization at home. And, *vice versâ*, the efforts of Christian philanthropy at home, by a natural expansiveness, lead to an active sympathy with all that is calculated to extend the blessings of Christianity to the uttermost ends of the earth.

But it is sometimes said that we ought not to send out missionaries to other countries until we have converted all our 'home heathen.' It is remarkable that this assertion is more often brought forward as an excuse for refusing to support the missionary cause than as an inducement to more strenuous support of evangelistic efforts at home. For what is the fact? those who take an interest in foreign missions have always been among those who most truly sympathize with, and most earnestly help forward 'home missions.' Moreover, a great fallacy is involved in the assertion that we are bound to confine our efforts at Christianizing to one place, until that place be thoroughly Christianized. The duty of the Christian is to be a witness for Christ in any and every place, as soon as, and as often as he can. He is to sow the good seed in the morning, and in the evening he is not to withhold his hand, uncertain whether shall prosper either this or that, or whether they shall both be alike good. The initiation of the work is confided as a privilege and a duty into his hands; but the furtherance of it to its final issue remains the sole prerogative of God. Christ bade his disciples be witnesses to Him 'in Jerusalem, in all Judæa, and Samaria, and unto the end of the earth[1].' They were not to confine themselves to one place; they were not to shut themselves up in the circle of their own neighbourhood and country, but to proclaim the glad message of the Saviour as widely as possible. Some would reject that message; but 'the gospel of the kingdom was to be preached in the whole habitable world for a witness unto all nations; and then should the end come[2].'

The individual Christian himself is not perfected upon earth. The great missionary Apostle at the end of his career confessed that 'he was not yet made perfect, and was still following on if that he might lay hold

---

[1] Acts i. 8.   [2] Matt. xxiv. 14.

of that for which he was laid hold of by Christ.' And such is the experience of every Christian as he advances in spiritual attainments. Is he, then, to wait until he himself be perfect before he make any endeavour to hold forth the word of life? Surely no one would maintain that this should be so. But the same principle must be further applied. Is a Christian to refuse to have anything to do with the amelioration of society before his own family and household are, in all respects, perfectly Christian? If he have the opportunity to help forward the proclamation of Christ's truth among those who know it not is he to say, 'There is much of ignorance and wickedness in London, therefore I will do nothing to remove the ignorance and wickedness which are found in India, and China, and the isles of the sea?'

Only one consideration could justify such a resolve; and that is, if by doing the one work he was preventing himself from going on with the other. But, on the contrary, as has been already said, the two works are mutually interdependent, and re-act, with beneficial results, the one upon the other. The blood which the heart sends to the extremities of the body goes and returns continually, keeping up that circulation of life without which the organism would become unhealthy and die.

Let there be no restriction upon the energy and enthusiasm of Christians, saving the humble sense of their own insufficiency and shortsightedness, which will prevent them from being impatient, and from expecting to see the harvest too soon after the seed has been cast into the ground. Let them all, in every way that they can, diffuse the light which they themselves have received; and, whether in their own country or in foreign lands, fulfil the work which Christ has given them to do for Him.

The propagation of Christ's religion, not in the pageantry of splendid ceremonies, not in any exclusive framework of denominational sectarianism, but in the simple and unfettered power of its mysterious and spiritual truths, here by one body of Christians, there by another, is the hope of the world. This alone can make wars to cease in the earth; this alone can verify the prescient words of prophets, and the pregnant dreams of poets, and usher in the kingdom of the Prince of Peace.

> "Were half the power that fills the world with terror,
>   Were half the wealth bestowed on camps and courts,
> Given to redeem the human mind from error,
>   There were no need of arsenals and forts.
>
> "The warrior's name would be a name abhorred!
>   And every nation that should lift again
> Its hand against a brother, on its forehead
>   Would wear for evermore the curse of Cain!
>
> " Down the dark future, through long generations,
>   The echoing sounds grow fainter and then cease,
> And, like a bell with solemn sweet vibrations,
>   I hear once more the voice of Christ say 'PEACE.'"

APPENDIX.

APPENDIX.

Note A. P. 13.

... "The Spanish commander added this formidable intimation from himself. He knew, he said, that Atahuallpa was a puissant monarch, and a great warrior; but his own master, the king of Spain, was sovereign of the entire world, and had a number of servants who were greater princes than Atahuallpa.....Pizarro then proceeded to account for his own presence there, saying that the emperor had sent him into that country to bring its inhabitants to the knowledge of God; and that, with the few Christians who accompanied him, he had already vanquished greater kings than Atahuallpa. The Spanish commander concluded by putting before the messengers an alternative. 'If,' he said, 'Atahuallpa wishes to be my friend, and to receive me as such, in the way that other princes have done, I will be his friend. ......If, on the other hand, he wishes for war, I will wage it against him.'"...

On the occasion of the interview which followed, Father Vicente de Valverde went forward with a cross in one hand, and a breviary in the other, and made an address to the Inca, which was divided into two parts. In the first part the speaker said that it was desirable that the king should recognize the necessity of being taught the true Catholic

Faith, and that he "should listen to and believe the following things. First, that God, three and one, created heaven and earth, and all things in the world; amongst them man, a creature who consists of body and rational soul." The Father then proceeded to speak very shortly concerning the sinfulness of man, and the history of Jesus Christ: and asserted that it was Christ's will that St Peter should be the prince of the Apostles and of their successors, and that he should be the Vicar of God; and that after him all the Roman Pontiffs should have the same supreme authority. Father Vicente then proceeded to the temporal part of his oration. "The Pope," he said, "who now lives upon earth (Father Vicente's history here halts a little, confounding Alexander the Sixth with Clement the Seventh, but, probably, he thought it the best way of explaining the matter to a barbarous monarch), understanding that all these nations (the Indians) had quitted the service of the true God and adored idols and likenesses of the Devil, and, wishing to bring them to the true knowledge of God, granted the conquest of these parts to Charles the Fifth, Emperor of the Romans, most powerful king of Spain, and monarch of the whole earth (here again the history would not have borne European criticism), in order that having conquered these nations, and cast out the rebels and obstinate persons from amongst them, he should govern these nations, bringing them to the knowledge of God and to the obedience of the Church." "Our most powerful king," the good Father went on to say, "although he was very much occupied in the government of his own kingdom, did not refuse this charge, and had accordingly sent his captains, who had subdued and brought to the true religion the great Islands and the country of Mexico. With these motives the powerful emperor, Charles the Fifth, has chosen for his lieutenant and ambassador Don Francisco Pizarro (who is here), that these kingdoms of your highness may receive the same benefits which those other lands have received (*at this moment there was scarcely an Indian left alive in Hispaniola*), and that an alliance of perpetual friendship should be made between his majesty and your highness." Father Vicente then explained what this alliance meant. It was, that Atahuallpa should pay tribute, renounce the administration of his kingdom, obey the Pope, believe in Jesus Christ, and give up idolatry. The priest concluded the temporal part of his oration with stern threats of fire and sword in case the Inca should not consent to this arrangement. "If with an obstinate mind you endeavour to resist," said Father Vicente, "you may take it for very certain that God will permit that, as anciently Pharaoh and all his army perished in the Red Sea, so you and all your Indians will be destroyed by our arms."

"That last sentence is a triumph of pedantry, furnishing an historical example which it was impossible for the Inca to know anything about, and prophesying in a manner that must have been unintelligible to him. The fulfilment of the prophecy was, however, near at hand; and Father Vicente can hardly be acquitted of having had some share in accelerating it."

Note B. P. 14.

"With respect to making war upon the Indians, they were to be carefully informed and to have thorough notice (*entera noticia*) of the danger they would run from war being once commenced, namely, of those taken alive being made slaves. For this purpose a document had been framed by Dr Palacios Rubios, a very learned jurist of that day and a member of the council......It went by the name of *El Requerimento* (the Requisition), and it ran thus:

"On the part of the king, Don Fernando, and of Doña Juana, his daughter, queen of Castille and Leon, subduers of the barbarous nations, we their servants notify and make known to you, as best we can, that the Lord our God, living and eternal, created the heaven and the earth, and one man and woman, of whom you and we, and all the men of the world, were and are descendants, and all those who come after us. But on account of the multitude which has sprung from this man and this woman in the five thousand years since the world was created, it was necessary that some men should go one way and some another, and that they should be divided into many kingdoms and provinces, for in one they could not be sustained. Of all these nations God our Lord gave charge to one man, called St Peter, that he should be lord and superior of all the men in the world, that all should obey him, and that he should be the head of the whole human race wherever men should live, and under whatever law, sect, or belief they should be; and he gave him the world for his kingdom and jurisdiction. And he commanded him to place his seat in Rome, as the spot most fitting to rule the world from; but also he permitted him to have his seat in any other part of the world, and to judge and govern all Christians, Moors, Jews, Gentiles, and all other sects. This man was called Pope, as if to say, Admirable Great Father and Governor of men. The men who lived in that time obeyed that St Peter and took him for lord, king, and superior of the universe" (imagine what Tiberius or Nero would have said to this assertion!); "so also they have regarded the others, who after him have been elected to the pontificate, and so has it been continued even until now, and will continue till the end of the world. One of these pontiffs, who succeeded that St Peter as lord of the world, in the dignity and seat which I have before mentioned, made donation of these isles and terra-firma to the aforesaid king, queen, and to their successors, our lords, with all that there are in these territories, as is contained in certain writings which passed upon the subject as aforesaid, which you can see if you wish. So their highnesses are kings and lords of these islands and land of terra-firma by virtue of this donation : and some islands, and indeed almost all those to whom this has been notified, have received and served their highnesses, as lords and kings, in the way that subjects ought to do, with goodwill, without any resistance, immediately, without delay, when they were informed of the aforesaid facts. And also they received and obeyed the priests whom their highnesses sent to preach to them and to teach them our holy faith ; and all these of their own free will, without any reward or condition, have become Christians and are so, and their highnesses have joyfully and benignantly received them, and have also commanded them to be treated as their subjects and vassals ; and you too are held and obliged to do the same. Wherefore, as best we can, we ask and require you that you should consider what we have said to you, and that you take the time that shall be necessary to understand and deliberate upon it, and that you acknowledge the Church as the ruler and superior of the whole world (*por Señora y Superiora del universo mundo*), and the high priest called Pope, and in his name the king and queen Doña Juana, our lords, in his place, as superiors and lords and kings of these islands and this terra-firma by virtue of the said donation, and that you consent and give place that these religious fathers should declare and preach to you the aforesaid. If you do so, you will do well, and that which you are obliged to do to their highnesses; and we in their name shall receive you in all love and charity, and shall leave you your wives, and your children, and your lands, free without servitude, that you may do with them and with yourselves freely that which you like and think best, and they shall not compel you to turn Christians unless you yourselves, when informed of the truth, should wish to be converted to our holy catholic faith, as almost all the inhabitants of the rest of the islands have done. And besides this, their highnesses award you many privileges and exemptions" (hard words in a new world!), "and will grant you many benefits. But if you do not do this, and maliciously make delay in it, I certify to you that, with the help of God, we shall powerfully enter into your country, and shall make war against you in all ways and manners that we can, and shall subject you to the yoke and obedience of the Church and of their highnesses; we shall take you and your wives and your children, and shall make slaves of them, and as such shall sell and dispose of them as their highnesses may command; and we shall take away your goods, and shall do you all the mischief and damage that we can, as to vassals who do not obey, and refuse to receive their lord, and resist and contradict him; and we protest that the deaths and losses which shall accrue from this are your fault, and not that of their highnesses or ours, nor of these cavaliers who come with us. And that we have said this to you and made this requisition, we request the notary here present to give his testimony in writing, and we ask the rest who are present that they should be witnesses of this requisition."......" I must confess (adds Mr Helps) that the comicality of this document has often cheered me in the midst of tedious research, or endless details of small battles. The logic, the history, even the grammatical construction are all, as it seems to me, alike in error. Stupendous assumptions are the staple of the document; and the very terms 'Church,' 'privileges,' 'vassalage,' 'exemptions,' are such as require a knowledge of Christianity and of the peculiar civilization of Europe for any one to understand. Then, when it is imagined how little these difficulties would be smoothed by translation, we may fancy what ideas the reading of this document, even when it was read, conveyed to a number of Indians sitting in a circle, and listening to European voices for the first time."

Note C. P. 15.

"The opinion which Bernardo de Mesa laid before the king was to the following effect:—That especial heed should be taken to convert the Indians; that they were not slaves but vassals; that 'for their own good' they must be ruled in some manner of servitude; that they had nothing but personal services to give; that idleness is the mother of all evil; that finally the Indians might be given in *encomienda*, but not to every Spaniard, only to those who were of good conscience and customs, and who besides employing the Indians who should be allotted to them would instruct them in matters of the faith...."

Note D. P. 21.

" A car approaches, covered with awnings of silk and decked with garlands of flowers. It is surmounted by a female statue, and dragged slowly by a tumultuous crowd. She bears the *tirubashi*, a ring through her nose, and the sacred nuptial collar round her neck.. On each side are parasol bearers, one who waves a napkin to brush away the mosquitoes. The car is preceded by dancers, half-naked, and streaked with sandal-wood powder and vermilion. Wild shouts ring through the air, and the ear is stunned by the din of trumpets, drums, and barbaric music. It is night; but amidst a general illumination and the blazing of torches innumerable, rockets, fireworks, ascend in every direction. The crowd is all Hindoos, and all bear on their foreheads the accustomed mark of idolaters. The car is the gift of a heathen prince, the dancers and music are borrowed from the nearest pagoda, the spectators are heathen, but *the woman represents the Virgin Mary, and the actors in this scandalous scene are the Christians of Madura.*"—*Calcutta Review*, Vol. II. 96.

Hough, in the passage cited, gives a very similar description of a procession at Pondicherry, and says that "throughout the procession neither prayers nor hymns were chanted, the whole being conducted, say the Romish missionaries of other orders [than the Jesuits], more like an idolatrous service than a Christian solemnity."

Steinmetz adds the following quotation from Dubois:

"The Hindoo pageantry is chiefly seen in the festivals celebrated by the native Christians. Their processions in the streets, always performed in the night time, have indeed been to me, at all times, a subject of shame. Accompanied with hundreds of *tom-toms* (small drums), trumpets, and all the discordant, noisy music of the country; with numberless torches and fireworks; the statue of the saint placed on a car which is laden with garlands of flowers, and other gaudy ornaments, according to the taste of the country; the car slowly dragged by a multitude shouting all along the march; the congregation surrounding the car, all in confusion, several among them dancing or playing with small sticks, or with naked swords: some wrestling, some playing the fool, all shouting or conversing with each other, without any one exhibiting the least sign of respect or devotion. Such is the mode in which the Hindoo Christians of the inland country celebrate their festivals." In fact Dubois expressly says, that "the first missionaries," i. e. the

Jesuits, "incumbered the Catholic worship with an additional superstructure of outward show, unknown in Europe, which, in many instances, does not differ much from that prevailing among the Gentiles, and which is far from proving a subject of edification to many a good and sincere Roman Catholic." Dubois' *Letters,* pp. 69, 70.

[The author of this essay remembers seeing a *Christian* procession at Madura, which, though on a smaller scale, was in the same manner as those above described essentially heathenish in all its main features. The crowd which followed the idol (in this case an image of the Virgin) were in all respects similar to the heathen; they bore the idolatrous marks; they were marching round a sacred 'tank,' in the midst of which was a heathen shrine; the dancing-girls and music from the heathen temple were there, and the only mark of Christianity that could be discerned was a cross held up near the image of the Virgin.]

The following passage from the *Lettres Édifiantes* (XI. 148), being the description given by a Jesuit of the manner in which he conducted a festival in honour of the Saviour, is worth quoting:

"La nuit du samedi ou dimanche je fis preparer un petit char de triomphe, que nous ornâmes de pièces de soi, de fleurs et de fruits. On y plaça l'image du Sauveur ressuscité, et le char fut conduit en triomphe par trois fois autour de l'église, au son de plusieur instruments. Les illuminations, les fusées volantes, les lances à feu, les girandoles et diverses autres feux d'artifice où les Indiens excellent, rendaient la fête magnifique......Le seigneur de la peuplade avec toute sa famille, et le reste des Gentiles qui assistèrent à la procession, se prosternèrent par trois fois devant l'image de Jésus ressuscité et *l'adorèrent* d'une manière qui les *confondait* heureusement avec les Chrétiens les plus fervens."

Note E. P. 25.

"Upper California was discovered by the Spaniards in 1543, and more than two hundred years after, viz. in 1767, they decided to settle and civilize it, the enterprize being entrusted to the care of the priesthood. A Franciscan friar was named Missionary President. San Diego, Monterey, and San Francisco, so called after the patron saint of the Franciscan order, were successively occupied. The system carried out was an enslavement of the aboriginal race to the temporal and spiritual despotism of the fathers; one so deteriorating in the influence which it exercised, that the population could only be sustained by proselytizing expeditions into the Indian territories, in which women and children were the first objects of capture, in the expectation that the husbands and parents would voluntarily follow them into captivity. The newly captured, according to the Franciscan mode, were as rapidly as possible converted into Christians. Captain Beechey, in 1826, thus describes the process: 'I happened to visit the Mission about this time, and saw these unfortunate beings under tuition. They were clothed in blankets, and arranged in a row before a blind Indian, who understood their dialect, and was assisted by an alcalde to keep order. Their tutor began by desiring them to kneel, informing them that he was going to teach them the names of the persons composing the Trinity, and that they were to repeat in Spanish what he dictated. The neophytes being thus arranged, the speaker began, "Santissima Trinidada, Dios, Jesu Christo, Espiritu Santo," pausing between each name to listen if the simple Indians, who had never spoken a Spanish word before, pronounced it correctly, or anything near the mark. After they had repeated these names satisfactorily, their blind tutor, after a pause, added

"Santos," and recapitulated the names of a great many saints, which finished the morning's tuition. After a few days, no doubt, these promising pupils were christened, and admitted to all the benefits and privileges of Christians and *gente de razon*. Indeed, I believe that the act of making the cross and kneeling at proper times, and other suchlike mechanical rites, constitute no small part of the religion of these poor people. The rapidity of the conversion is, however, frequently stimulated by practices much in accordance with the primary kidnapping of the subjects. If, as not unfrequently happens, any of the captured Indians show a repugnance to conversion, it is the practice to imprison them for a few days, and then to allow them to breathe a little fresh air in a walk round the Mission, to observe the happy mode of life of their converted countrymen; after which they are again shut up, and thus continue incarcerated until they declare their readiness to renounce the religion of their forefathers. As might be believed, the ceremonial exercises of the Roman Catholic religion occupy a considerable share of the time of these people. Mass is performed twice daily, besides high days and holidays, when the ceremonies are much grander, and of longer duration; and at all the performances every Indian is obliged to attend, under the penalty of a whipping; and this same method of enforcing proper discipline, as in kneeling at proper times, keeping silence, &c., is not excluded from the church service itself. In the aisles and passages of the church, zealous beadles of the converted race are stationed, armed with sundry weapons of potent influence in effecting silence and attention, and which are not sparingly used on the refractory or inattentive. These consist of sticks and whips, long goads, &c., and they are not idle in the hands of the officials that sway them.'"— *Church Missionary Intelligencer* (1858), pp. 220, 221.

"With other hordes the fathers thought themselves fortunate in obtaining permission to visit the prisoners, and instruct them in saving faith before they were put to death. But the savages soon took a conceit that the water of baptism spoilt the taste of the meat, and therefore would not let them baptize them any more. The Jesuits then carried with them wet handkerchiefs, or contrived to wet the skirt or sleeve of their habit, that out of it they might squeeze water enough upon the victim's head to fulfil the condition of salvation, without which they were persuaded that eternal fire must have been his portion. What will not man believe, if he can believe this of his Maker?

"If the missionaries, overcoming all difficulties, succeeded in converting a clan at last, that conversion was so little the effect of reason or feeling, that any slight circumstance would induce the proselytes to relapse into their old paganism. An epidemic disorder appeared among them; they said it was occasioned by the water of baptism, and all the converts whom Nobrega and his fellow-labourers had with such difficulty collected would have deserted them and fled into the woods, if he had not pledged his word that the malady should cease. Luckily for him it was effectually cured by bleeding, a remedy to which they were unaccustomed. Some time afterwards a cough and catarrh cut off many of them; this also was attributed to baptism. The Jesuits themselves did not ascribe greater powers to this ceremony than they did; whatever calamity befel them was readily accounted for by these drops of mysterious water. Many tribes have supposed it fatal to children; the eagerness with which the missionaries baptize the dying, and especially new-born infants who are not likely to live, have occasioned this notion." Southey, *History of Brazil*, c. VIII.

Adam Schall, the famous Jesuit missionary in China,

when some twenty guns had been made for the emperor under his instructions, "consecrated," we are told, "the glorious achievement with Christian rites and ceremonies—anticipating the Chinamen who were about to offer sacrifice to the Spirit of Fire...The Jesuit brought forth an image of Christ, placed it upon an altar which he had raised and ornamented for the purpose, and went through a ceremonial veneration, dressed in his surplice and stole. He ordered the workmen to do the same on bended knee to call down the Divine assistance upon the labour. The emperor commanded his people to do as the Jesuit prescribed in this matter, as well as in all others, and rigorously forbade any resistance to his wishes; 'for,' said he, and the words are remarkable, 'these men [the Jesuits] *do not despise the spirits whom we adore:* but they tenaciously worship one God, and observe his laws.'" Steinmetz, III. 408.

The Jesuits were in the habit of baptizing exposed infants in China, and adding them to the number of their converts. Thus "Father Gaubil, in a letter from Pekin in 1726," said that the Jesuits there baptized "annually 3000 exposed infants." And Steinmetz, referring to this practice, says afterwards: "Two thousand five hundred in two years thus went to heaven," *sont allés au ciel;* and but for the persecution the work would have been regularly set on foot in several large towns, and in a few years "we would have sent to heaven more than 20000 little children per annum; *on aurait envoyé par an dans le ciel plus de vingt mille petits enfans.*"

Note F. P. 33.

"Father Luis Cancer had been one of the Dominicans engaged with Las Casas in his peaceful conquest of the 'Land of War.' Indeed, he was the first monk who had entered that territory; and it was upon his report that the others had been emboldened to persevere in their attempt. Father Luis had hoped to convert the natives of Florida in the same manner that he had converted the inhabitants of Coban. Unfortunately, however, he landed in Florida at a spot where the natives had suffered from the incursions of hostile Spaniards, and the devoted monk was put to death by the Indians almost immediately after he had disembarked. This was a valuable fact for Sepulveda, who accordingly made use of it in the controversy.

"The dignity and greatness of his cause were so predominant in the mind of Las Casas as to leave no room for influences merely personal. It does not appear that he ever expected gratitude from the Indians; nor did the terrible disaster which he suffered at Cumaná from the treachery of the natives leave, apparently, the slightest rancour in his mind. His reply to Sepulveda, respecting Luis Cancer's death, was as follows: 'The first person who entered into those territories and pacified them, was brother Luis, of happy memory, who was afterwards slain in Florida, and of whose death the reverend doctor, Sepulveda, desires to avail himself in argument. But it avails him little; for if they had slain all the brotherhood of St Dominic, and St Paul with them, not a point of right would have been attained more than there had been before (which was none) against the Indians. The cause of his death was that in that port where he was taken by those sinners of mariners (who ought to have landed elsewhere, as they were instructed) there had entered and disembarked four armadas of cruel tyrants who had perpetrated extraordinary cruelties amongst the Indians of those lands, and had alarmed, scandalised, and devastated a thousand leagues of the country. On this account they will have a most just cause of war against the

Spaniards, and indeed against all Christians even to the day of judgment. And as these Floridians had no knowledge of monks, and had never seen them, they could not divine that they were missionaries, especially as they were in the company of those who were exactly like in manners, dress, beards, and language, to the persons who had done them so much mischief, and the natives saw them eat, drink, and laugh together as friends.'"

NOTE G. P. 35.

Anacaona was the queen of a district in Hispaniola called Xaragua. She and her people had consented to pay tribute to the Spaniards, and until Ovando became governor of the Spanish colony had lived in peace and amity with the Spaniards. Herrera, in his *History of the Indies*, says "that Anacaona's people were in policy, in language, and in other things superior to all the other inhabitants of the island." In 1503 several Spaniards settled in Xaragua, and gave much trouble to the governing powers of that province. Disturbances arose, "and the Spaniards took care to inform the governor that their adversaries the Indians of Xaragua intended to rebel." Ovando, thereupon, determined upon a visit to Xaragua. He took with him 70 horsemen and 300 foot soldiers. Anacaona "went out to meet Ovando with a concourse of her subjects, and with the same festivities of singing and dancing as in former days she had adopted when she went to receive the Adelantado [in 1497]. Various pleasures and amusements were provided for the strangers, and probably Anacaona thought that she had succeeded in soothing and pleasing the severe looking governor, as she had done the last." But the Spaniards, using "those seemingly wise arguments of wickedness which from time immemorial have originated and perpetuated treachery," persuaded Ovando that an insurrection was intended. And so Ovando "ordered that on a certain Sunday, after dinner, all the cavalry should get to horse, on the pretext of a tournament. The infantry, too, he caused to be ready for action. He himself, a Tiberius in dissembling, went to play at quoits, and was disturbed by his men coming to him and begging him to look on at their sports. The poor Indian queen hurried with the utmost simplicity into the snare prepared for her. She told the governor that the caciques too would like to see this tournament, upon which, with demonstrations of pleasure, he bade her come with all her caciques to his quarters, for he wanted to talk to them, intimating, as I conjecture, that he would explain the festivity to them. Meanwhile he gave his cavalry orders to surround the buildings; he placed the infantry at certain commanding positions; and told his men, that when, in talking to the caciques, he should place his hand upon the badge of knighthood which hung upon his breast, they should rush in and bind the caciques and Anacaona. It fell out as he had planned. All these deluded Indian chiefs and their queen were secured. She alone was led out of Ovando's quarters, *which were then set fire to, and all the chiefs burnt alive. Anacaona was afterwards hanged,* and the province was desolated....Finally the governor collected the former followers of Roldan in Xaragua, and formed a town of their settlement, which he named "the city of true peace" (*La ville de la vera Paz*), but which a modern chronicler well says might more properly have been named "Aceldama, the field of blood." "I observe," adds Mr Helps, "that the arms assigned to this settlement were *a dove with the olive branch, a rainbow, a cross.*" Thus deeds of cold-blooded treachery and cruel murder were signed with the Christian symbols of peace, hope, and love!

The other passage alluded to relates the treachery by which the Spanish discoverer of the South Sea, Vasco Nuñez, invaded the territory of the cacique Careta. It appears that two Spaniards had some time before deserted their ship and had been received kindly by this cacique of Cueva. One of them, indeed, Juan Alonso, (whom Las Casas, in his narrative of the treachery perpetrated, likens to Judas Iscariot) had been made the Indian chief's principal captain. Some of Nuñez' soldiers on their way to Darien met these two men "without clothes and painted, like the Indians." Juan Alonso "bade the Spaniards tell Vasco Nuñez that if he would come to Careta's town, he, Juan Alonso, would deliver his master, the cacique, bound, into the hands of Vasco Nuñez; and he also gave the alluring intelligence that there were great riches in that province."

"Vasco Nuñez was delighted at this news, and he prepared at once to act upon it, entering Careta's territories at the head of a hundred and thirty men. Having arrived with his 'apostles' as LAS CASAS calls them, at the Indian town where Careta dwelt, he found the cacique awaiting his coming. Vasco Nuñez, conscious of the treachery he was about to commit, and perhaps not liking to gild it over with fair words, rudely demanded provisions from the cacique. The Indian chief replied that, whenever Christians had passed by his home he had ordered provisions to be given them liberally, and he would do so now; at the same time he remarked that he was straitened himself, as he was at war with a neighbouring chief, Poncha, and his own people had not been able to sow as usual.

"Juan Alonso, probably speaking in Spanish in presence of the cacique, then suggested to Vasco Nuñez to pretend to take leave of the chief, and afterwards to come back at night in order to make an attack on the town; he, for his part, would do his best to secure the person of the cacique. Vasco Nuñez adopted the suggestion. He went away, but, returning at night, made his attack in three divisions, awakening the sleeping Indians with the war-cry of 'Santiago.'

"Juan Alonso, true to his promises of treachery, secured the person of the cacique; and Vasco Nuñez thus succeeded in carrying him and his family to Darien, and in devastating his town."

Note H. P. 47.

"There is no record," says Mr Philips, "remaining to show the district to which the first commando was sent, or how long it continued in the field; but it appears that the party engaged in this service, in the month of September, 1774, in the space of eight days succeeded in shooting ninety-six Bushmen. The women and children taken prisoners were divided among the men, but their number is not specified in the official report. Van Wyk was the name of the commandant. The second commando was conducted by a Boor named Marais. In his report to the Colonial Office, he states that he had taken one hundred and eighteen prisoners, who, it is presumed, must have been women and children, but the number killed is not mentioned. The third commando, under Vander Merve, was commissioned to the Bokkeveld, when they destroyed one hundred and forty-two Bushmen. Whether his humanity was shocked at his sanguinary employment, the duration of which to fulfil the purposes of government must then have appeared indefinite, or whether he dreaded their superior numbers, is uncertain; but, in violation of his instructions, he concluded a peace with the remaining chiefs. The government, on hearing of this transaction, highly resented it, and degraded all the field-cornets who had concurred with him in the measure. And in the following year these expeditions appear to have been repeated twice; one, on the 12th of June, succeeded in killing forty-eight of the devoted Bushmen, and would have followed up the carnage had not their numbers been insufficient. The number of wounded would, in all likelihood, greatly exceed that of the slain on these occasions, as they never ceased to run or scramble among the rocks in search of hiding places, till life forsook them; appearing to dread being taken more than death itself."

In the journal of Van Jaarsveld referred to, the Bushmen are continually called "thieves," and it is evident that the idea entertained by this commandant of the expedition was that the Bushmen, as thieves, were to be extirpated. The first entry quoted is as follows:

"*August* 4, 1775. We proceeded in a north-east direction to the upper end of the Sea-cow River, when we met, unawares, one of these cattle plunderers, and also saw a great many of these thieves at a distance. In order to create no suspicion in the mind of the thief whom we had caught, we behaved peaceably to him in order to get the other thieves in our power. Wherefore it was thought good by every one in the commando to inform this Bushman, that we came as friends and were only journeying to the above-mentioned river to kill sea-cows (Hippopotami). We gave him a pipe and tobacco, and sent him to his companions *to offer them our peace*, that they also might come to us to show us the right road to that river. But we have not seen that thief since."

After some difficulty, in spite of his bribes of hippopotamus flesh, Van Jaarsveld succeeded in finding out, by means of spies, a place on the river where some Bushmen had assembled to hunt the hippopotami in the night time. "About midnight," the journal continues, "the spies returned, saying they had seen a great number of Bushmen there, when I immediately repaired thither with the commando, waiting till day-break, which soon appeared; and having divided the commando into two parties, we slew the thieves, and, on searching, found one hundred and twenty-two dead; five escaped by swimming across the river."

Mr Philips, in the first chapter of his second volume, shows that the deterioration of the Bushmen is to be attributed to the savage and iniquitous treatment of them by their European oppressors: and he rightly remarks, "When savage and barbarous tribes are oppressed by civilized nations, perfidy and injustice are the only things they borrow from their oppressors; and the animosity excited by a sense of the injuries they sustain presents an insuperable barrier to their civilization."

Mr Philips gives extracts from letters in 1821 and 1822 to show that even then the commando system was being continued.

Note J. P. 49.

"The deposition of Uithaalder, the Captain of Toverberg:

"1st, That deponent is a chief of a tribe of the Bushman nation lying around Toverberg, south of the Great River, in the district of Graaf Reinet.

"2nd, That many years ago, the father of deponent and his people, whilst in perfect peace, and not having committed the smallest provocation, were suddenly attacked in their kraal by a party of Boors from the colony. He and many hundreds of his people, men, women, and children, were killed, and ten waggons, loaded with their children, were carried into the colony and placed in perpetual servitude.

"3rd, That since this melancholy occurrence many commandoes have come against my people, in which multitudes of them have been shot, and the children carried away: and this practice was continued till our late teacher, the Rev. E. Smith [a missionary of the London Missionary Society sent out in 1814], condescended to live among us, to preach the word of God, and to teach us to read, and to refrain from doing harm to anybody.

"4th, That while the Rev. E. Smith continued among us he taught us to cultivate gardens, he gave us seeds to plant them, he showed us how to grow potatoes, and ploughed land which he sowed for us; and when the harvest came, he taught us to cut down the corn and divided it among us; and as no more commandoes came against us we were very happy, and hoped that our troubles were over, and we should live in peace.

"5th, That while we were thus enjoying peace, and getting food to eat, the Rev. Mr Smith was commanded by the government of the colony to leave Toverberg; and the teacher was very much grieved, and many Bushmen's hearts were sore pained: we wept much, but remained on the land of our forefathers, cultivating our gardens, and praying to the great God for Mr Smith's return.

"6th, That some moons after Mr Smith's removal, the Boors came and took possession of our fountains, chased us from the lands of Toverberg, and made us go and keep their sheep. Whitboy, one of my Bushmen, and his wife, were both shot by the Boors whilst taking shelter among the rocks, and their child carried into perpetual servitude.

"7th, That I, Uithaalder, was sent by the field-cornet, Van der Walt, to keep his sheep; that one night three of his sheep were missing, and the field-cornet flogged deponent with the sambok, and drove himself and his wife and children from the place, and said, 'Go now, take that; you have not now Mr Smith, the missionary, to go to, to complain against me.'

"8th, That deponent then went to a small fountain near Toverberg, where a few Bushmen once lived; but that last moon the field-cornet drove himself and wife and young children from the fountain, saying, 'that Bushmen should have no fountains in this country, and that they should have no pools but the rain-water pools out of which to drink.'

"9th, That about ten moons ago Louw Styns, the son of Hans Styns, travelled with his cattle over the Great River; that I, Uithaalder, was watcher of his cattle, and one evening, when bringing the cattle home, some of the cattle were missing, when deponent was severely beaten with a stave by Louw Styns, who said, 'You have not Mr Smith to go to now.' The strayed cattle that evening came home of themselves; yet three different times was I beat by Louw Styns for the same reason, whereupon deponent left his service.

"10th, That I, Uithaalder, without people, with my wife and four young children, was necessitated to live among the mountains, and to subsist upon roots and locusts; and that, on hearing from a Bushman, who knew where deponent and his family were gone to, that missionaries were at Toverberg, deponent came to their waggons on the road, and stated to them his case.

"Uithaalder humbly begs that such white men as are true Christians will take into consideration his distressing case, and the distressing situation of his countrymen who have survived the murdering commandoes, and who, after having been deprived of their fountains, their gardens, and their game, are obliged to see their children taken from them, and themselves driven among wild beasts.

"11th, That last moon, whilst I, Uithaalder, ventured out to the plains, seeking roots to eat, a Boor came up to deponent, and inquired what I was doing there? saying that I meant to steal some of his sheep, and eat them; and he, the Boor, beat your deponent with a sambok severely over the head.

"12th, That Uithaalder knows that much has been said against the Bushmen. Whenever sheep, or goats, or cattle have either strayed, or been stolen, the Boors say the Bushmen have stolen them, and they are flogged, and shot, on suspicion only, for the cattle and sheep which have been taken by others, or destroyed by the lions, wolves, and tigers.

"13th, That Uithaalder allows that Bushmen may, when starving, have taken a sheep from a farmer's flock, to keep himself and children alive, but deponent is certain that this seldom happens, and that the Bushmen are blamed and punished without having done anything wrong; and, as a proof of this assertion, he may state, that three sheep for which he was flogged and driven from the field-cornet's place were found next day."

Note K. P. 63.

"The general account of our intercourse with the North American Indians, as distinct from missionary efforts, may be given in the words of a converted Chippeway chief, in a letter to Lord Goderich: 'We were once very numerous, and owned all Upper Canada, and lived by hunting and fishing; but the white men who came to trade with us taught our fathers to drink the fire-waters, which has made our people poor and sick, and has killed many tribes, till we have become very small.'" Howitt, p. 381.

Dr O'Meara said, "I will mention another fact in reference to the effect of the character of Europeans on the natives in their own country. I remember an Indian chief on Lake Huron, who had given special opposition to the Christian work amongst his people. I visited him, and I spoke my mind to him very freely, telling him that it was not so much a love of his own superstitions, as a love of the fire-water, that made him dislike the mission; that he wished to have his young men join him in his drunken frolics; and did not wish them to become Christians, for he knew that if they became Christians they would cease from such doings. I shall never forget the way in which that Indian chief drew himself up to his full height, and the look of scorn with which he regarded me when he said, 'Is it you, a white man, who address me in that style? Who brought the fire-water to us? We knew nothing of it till you came amongst us; we ate the flesh of the deer; and when we had got enough of that, we went to the edge of the lakes and rivers and drank our fill, and it did us no harm: but you white men came with this fire-water in your hands. We thought it strange, bad medicine, at first; but you told us that it would do us good, make us happy and joyful, and we took it and drank it. It did make us very happy and joyful; and since then we have liked it, and we will have it whenever we can get it. If you want us not to take the fire-water, go and tell your own people so. We cannot make the fire-water; if they don't make it, we cannot get it; and if they don't bring it amongst us, your work is done: but teach your own people about it first.' There is another matter also I would wish to mention. It has often been said that commerce is the handmaid of religion; but I am sorry to say, that amongst the North American Indians commerce has proved the enemy of religion, and the missionary has often to become the enemy of the trader. The trader finds, that when the Indians are Christianized they become civilized; that their minds are improved; that they begin to know the value of their own wares; that he cannot carry on so profitable a trade; and therefore he hates and abhors the progress of Christianity because he cannot put so much of this world's pelf in his own pocket. The missionary, therefore, has often to stand in opposition to the trader, in the defence of those whom the trader injures in their temporal prosperity."

Note L. P. 78.

The capitan's name was Mancio Sierra de Leguizamo. He thus expresses himself in his will:—" We found these kingdoms governed in such a manner that throughout them there was not a thief, nor idler, nor a vicious man; neither was there any adulterous or bad woman. The lands, the mountains, the mines, the pastures, the houses, the woods, were governed and divided in such a manner that each man knew and kept to his own estate. There were no law-suits about property..." He then says that the Spaniards (speaking of himself as one of them) *have destroyed, with their bad example,* people of such good government as these nations of Peru were...;" and deplores that the extremely innocent and unsuspicious condition of the Peruvians "has been changed, by bad example, into nothing good being done by them. He asks from the king a remedy for these evils, and, as the last of the conquerors left alive, thus discharges his conscience by setting forth, in a solemn instrument to be communicated to his majesty, the state of things in Peru which it concerned *the king's soul to know as well as his own soul to declare.*"

Note M. P. 81.

"But the most singular feature of the treatment of the Indians by the Americans is, that while they assign their irreclaimable nature as the necessary cause of their expelling or desiring to expel them from all the states east of the Mississippi, their most strenuous and most recent efforts have been directed against those numerous tribes, that were not only extensive, but rapidly advancing in civilization. So far from refusing to adopt settled, orderly habits, the Choctaws, Chickasaws, Creeks, and Cherokees, were fast conforming both to the religion and the habits of the Americans. The Creeks were numbered in 1814 at 20,000. The Choctaws had some years ago 4041 warriors, and could not therefore be estimated at less than four times that number in total population, or 16,000. In 1810, the Cherokees consisted of 12,400 persons; in 1824 they had increased to 15,000. The Chickasaws reckoned some years ago 1000 warriors, making the tribe probably 4000.

"The Creeks had twenty years ago cultivated lands, flocks, cattle, gardens, and different kinds of domestic manufactures. They were betaking themselves to manual trades and farming. 'The Choctaws,' Mr Stuart says, 'have both schools and churches. A few books have been published in the Choctaw language. In one part of their territory, where the population amounted to 5627 persons, there were above 11,000 cattle, about 4000 horses, 22,000 hogs, 530 spinning-wheels, 360 ploughs, etc.' The missionaries speak in the highest terms of their steadiness and sobriety; and one of their chiefs had actually offered himself as a candidate for Congress. All these tribes are described as rapidly progressing in education and civilization, but the Cherokees present a character which cannot be contemplated without the liveliest admiration. These were the tribes amongst whom Adair spent so many years, about the middle of the last century, and whose customs and ideas as delineated by him, exhibited them as such fine material for cultivation. Since then the missionaries, and especially the Moravians, have been labouring with the most signal success. A school was opened in this tribe by them in 1804, in which vast numbers of Cherokee children have been educated. Such, indeed, have been the effects of cultivation on this fine people, that they have assumed all the habits and pursuits of civilized life. Their progress may be noted by observing the amount of their possessions in 1810, and again, fourteen years afterwards, in 1824. In the former year they had 3 schools, in the latter 18; in the former year 13 grist-mills, in the latter 36; in the former year 3 saw-mills, in the latter 13; in the former year 467 looms, in the latter 762; in the former year 1,600 spinning-wheels, in the latter 2,486; in the former year 30 wagons, in the latter 172; in the former year 500 ploughs, in the latter 2,923; in the former year 6,100 horses, in the latter 7,683; in the former year 19,500 head of cattle, in the latter 22,531; in the former year 19,600 swine, in the latter 46,732; in the former year 1,037 sheep, in the latter 2,546, and 430 goats; in the former year 49 smiths, in the latter 62 smiths' shops. Here is a steady and prosperous increase; testifying to no ordinary existence of industry, prudence, and good management amongst them, and bearing every promise of their becoming a most valuable portion of the community. They have, Mr Stuart tells us, several public roads, fences, and turnpikes. The soil produces maize, cotton, tobacco, wheat, oats, indigo, sweet and Irish potatoes. The natives carry on a considerable trade with the adjoining states, and some of them export cotton to New Orleans. Apple and peach orchards are common, and gardens well cultivated. Butter and cheese are the produce of their dairies. There are many houses of public entertainment kept by the natives. Numerous and flourishing villages are seen in every section of the country. Cotton and woollen cloths and blankets are everywhere. Almost every family in the nation produces cotton for its own consumption. Nearly all the nation are native Cherokees.

"A printing-press has been established for several years; and a newspaper, written partly in English, and partly in Cherokee, has been successfully carried on. This paper, called the *Cherokee Phœnix*, is written entirely by a Cherokee, a young man under thirty. It had been surmised that he was assisted by a white man, on which he put the following notice in the paper:—'No white has anything to do with the management of our paper. No other person, whether white or red, besides the ostensible editor, has written, from the commencement of the *Phœnix*, half a column of matter which has appeared under the editorial head[1].'"

"The starting of this Indian newspaper by an Indian is one of the most interesting facts in the history of civilization. In this language nothing had been written or printed. It had no written alphabet. This young Indian, already instructed by the missionaries in English literature, is inspired with a desire to open the world of knowledge to his countrymen in their vernacular tongue. There is no written character, no types. Those words familiar to all native ears have no corresponding representation to the eye. These are gigantic difficulties to the young Indian, and, as the Christian would call him, *savage* aspirant and patriot. But he determines to conquer them all. He travels into the eastern states. He invents letters which shall best express the sounds of his native tongue; he has types cut, and com-

[1] Stuart's *Three Years in North America*, II. 177.

mences a newspaper. There is nothing like it in the history of nations in their first awakening from the long fixedness of wild life. This mighty engine, the press, once put in motion by native genius in the western wilderness, books are printed suitable to the nascent intelligence of the country. The Gospel of St Matthew is translated into Cherokee, and printed at the native press. Hymns are also translated and printed. Christianity makes rapid strides. The pupils in the schools advance with admirable rapidity. There is a new and wonderful spirit abroad. Not only do the Indians throng to the churches to listen to the truths of life and immortality, but Indians themselves become diligent ministers, and open places of worship in the more remote and wild parts of the country. Even temperance societies are formed...

"The whole growth and being, however, of this young Indian civilization is one of the most delightful and animating subjects of contemplation that ever came before the eye of the lover of his race. Here were these Indian savages, who had been two hundred years termed irreclaimable; whom it had been the custom only to use as the demons of carnage, as creatures fit only to carry the tomahawk and the bloody scalping-knife through Cherry-Valley, Gnadenhuetten, or Wyoming; and whom, that work done, it was declared, must be cast out from the face of civilized man, as the reproach of the past and the incubus of the future,—here were they gloriously vindicating themselves from those calumnies and wrongs, and assuming in the social system a most beautiful and novel position. It was a spectacle on which one would have thought the United States would hang with a proud delight, and point to as one of the most noble features of their vast and noble country. What did they do? They chose rather to give the lie to all their assertions, that they drove out the Indians because they were irreclaimable and unamalgamable, and to shew to the world that they expelled them solely and simply because they scorned that one spot of the copper hue of the aborigines should mar the whiteness of their population."

NOTE N. P. 89.

The title of the book by Terry referred to in the note is, 'A VOYAGE to EAST INDIA; wherein Some Things are taken Notice of, In our PASSAGE THITHER, But MANY MORE in our ABODE THERE within that RICH and most SPACIOUS EMPIRE of the GREAT MOGUL, mixt with some Parallel Observations and Inferences upon the Story to profit as well as delight the READER.

Observed by EDWARD TERRY, then Chaplain to the Right Hon. Sir THOMAS ROW, Knt. Lord Ambassador to the Great Mogul.'

The edition from which I quote the following passages is one published in 1777, reprinted from the edition of 1655:

"When my Lord Ambassador at first arrived at Surat, it so was, that an English cook he carried with him, the very first day of his coming thither found a way to an Armenian Christian's house, who sold wine in that place, they call Armenian wine. But (by the way) I do believe there was scarce another in that populous city of that trade, the greater shame for those whosoever they be, that suffer so many unnecessary tipling houses, (in the places where they have power to restrain them) which are the devils nursery, the very tents wherein Satan dwells, where Almighty God receives abundance of dishonour; drunkenness being a sin which hath hands and fingers to draw all other sins into it; for a drunkard can do any thing, or be any thing but good. That Armenian wine I speak of is made of raisons of the sun and sugar, with some other things put and boiled in water; which wine when it is ripe and clear, is in colour like our Muscadels, pleasant enough to the taste but heavy and heady. The cook had his head quickly over-freighted with it, and then staggering homeward, in his way met the governor's brother of Surat, as he was riding to his house; the cook made a stand, staying himself up upon his sword and scabbard, and cry'd out to the governor's brother *Now thou heathen dog*. He not understanding his foul language, reply'd civily in his own, *Ca-ca-ta*, which signifies what say'st thou? the cook answered him with his sword and scabbard, with which he struck him, but was immediately seized on by his followers, and by them disarmed and carried to prison; the Ambassador had present intelligence of the misbehaviour of his drunken servant, and immediately sent word unto the governor's brother, that he was not come thither to patronise any disorderly person, and therefore desir'd him to do with him what he pleased; upon which he presently sent him home, not doing him the least hurt. But before I leave this story, it will not be amiss to enquire who was the *heathen dog* at this time; whether the debauch'd drunken cook, who call'd himself a Christian, or that sober and temperate Mahometan who was thus affronted."

A little further on, in the same chapter, the narrative proceeds as follows:

"After this, when we had gone forward about twenty days journey, (which daily removes were but short, by reason of our heavy carriages, and the heat of the weather) it happened that another of our company, a young gentleman about twenty years old, the brother of a baron of England, behaved himself so ill as that we feared it would have brought very much mischief on us......... But in our way towards that court, it thus happened that this hot-brains being a little behind us, commanded him then near him, who was the prince's servant, before spoken of, to hold his horse; the man reply'd, that he was none of his servant, and would not do it. Upon which this most intemperate mad youth, who was like Philocles that angry poet, and therefore called *bilis et salsigo* choler and brine, for he was the most hasty and cholerick young man that ever I knew, as will appear by his present carriage, which was thus; first he beat that stranger, for refusing to hold his horse, with his horse-whip, which I must tell you that people cannot endure, as if those whips stung worse than scorpions; for of any punishments that carry most disgrace in them, as that people think, one is to be beaten with that whip wherewith they strike their beasts; the other to be beaten (and this they esteem the more disgraceful punishment of the two) about the head with shoes. But this stranger (being whipt as before) came up and complained to me; but to make him amends, that frantick young man (mad with rage and he knew not wherefore) presently followed him, and being come up close to him, discharged his pistol laden with a brace of bullets directly at his body; which bullets by the 'special guidance of the hand of God, so flew, that they did the poor man no great hurt; only one of them, first tearing his coat, bruised all the knuckles of his left hand, and the other broke his bow which he carried in the same hand. We presently disarmed our young Bedlam, till he might return again to his wits. But our greatest business was how to pacify the other man, whom he had thus injured: I presently gave him a roopee, in our money two shillings and ninepence; he thanked me for it, and would have taken it with his right hand, but I desired him to take it with his maim'd one, and so he did, and could clinch it very well, which I was glad of. Then we did shew (as we had cause) all the dislike we could against that desperate act of him from whom he received his hurt, telling him that we were all strangers, and for our parts had done him no wrong at all, and therefore hoped that we should not be made any way to suffer for the faults of another; and we further told him that if he would be quiet 'till we came up to the court, he should have all the satisfaction he could desire. He told us we were good men, and had done him no wrong, and that he would 'till then rest contented; but he did not so, for about two hours after we met with a great man of that country, having a mighty train with him, as all the grandees there have when they travel (of whom more hereafter). He presently went towards him, that to him he might make his complaint; and so he did, telling him that he was the prince's servant, why he came to us, and how he had been used by us, shewing him his hand and his other breaches. The great man replied, that it was not well done of us, but he had nothing to do with it, and so departed on his way. That night after we came to a strong large town, and placing ourselves one side of it, he did what he could (as we imagined) to raise up that people against us, some of them coming about us to view us, as we conceived; but putting on the best confidence we could, and standing then upon our guard, and all of us watching that night, but in a 'special manner, by the good providence of God, who kept us in all our journey, we here felt none of that mischief we feared, but early in the morning quietly departed without the least molestation. After which, with a little money, and a great many good words, we so quieted this man, that we never after heard any more complaining from him. So that as I before observed we were not at any time in dangers of suffering by that people, but some of our own nation were the procuring causes of it."

Note O. P. 91.

In a pamphlet entitled, *The Indian Crisis: A memorial to the Queen from the Church Missionary Society, with an explanatory statement,*" &c., published in 1858, the whole subject of the government policy of *neutrality* is treated with great ability and soberness of argument from the missionary point of view.

The first of the following extracts from the *Church Missionary Intelligencer* will serve to show the contrast between the policy of toleration, and of hostility to Christian missions, which was brought out in the struggles which took place at the end of the last and the beginning of the present century between those who advocated and those who condemned missionary efforts in our Indian possessions.

The second contains the views of some American missionaries, in a work published soon after the mutiny of 1857.

An extract from Kaye's *Christianity in India* is subjoined, as bearing upon the historical view of the "Government connexion with idolatry."

"Our Government in India has been afflicted, from its commencement, with an excessive fear of interfering with the religion of the natives, lest their prejudices should be offended, and the quietude of our rule be disturbed. So powerful has this apprehensiveness been, that, previously to the renewal of the Company's charter in 1813, our policy was antagonistic to the free action of the gospel, and its extension amongst the natives of India. The times of the renewing of the Company's charter have been the seasons when the question has been most powerfully agitated. The resolutions of the British House of Commons in 1793 were becoming the dignity and position of a Christian legislature—'Resolved, That it is the opinion of this House, that it is the peculiar and bounden duty of the legislature to promote, by all just and prudent means, the interests and happiness of the inhabitants of the British dominions in India; and that, for these ends, such measures ought to be adopted as may gradually tend to their advancement in useful knowledge, and to their religious and moral improvement.' That resolution embodied the principle and germ of all that the friends of missions have ever wished for or proposed. But several proprietors of East-India Stock were violently opposed to the line of conduct here indicated; and, at a public meeting, the resolutions of the Commons' House were violently impugned, the objections which were urged, when stated, generally amounted to this—'That sending missionaries into our Eastern territories, is the most wild, extravagant, expensive, unjustifiable project that ever was suggested by the most visionary speculator; that the principle is obnoxious, impolitic, unnecessary, full of mischief, dangerous, useless, unlimited. The plan would be dangerous and impolitic; it would affect the peace and ultimate security of our possessions. It tends to endanger and injure our affairs there most fatally; it would either produce disturbances, or bring the Christian religion into contempt,' &c. We are disposed to think that some are to be met with, at the present day, whose opinions are so far behind the age, that in the above *resumé* they would not discover much to which they could not readily subscribe."

The testimony of some American missionaries on the subject, as cited in the *Church Missionary Intelligencer*, October, 1859, is as follows:

"There can be no doubt that the whole spirit of Government has been to pet and patronize superstitions, and to discourage every attempt to disturb or alter them. Toleration and neutrality have been the avowed views, and its settled policy was non-interference in religious matters; and there can be no question but that this was, all things taken into consideration, the best and wisest plan that could be adopted. But then the polity was one thing, and the practice quite another, and quite different. According to the latter, Government lent its aid and influence to the support and encouragement of idolatry and false religion; for not only were grants made to heathen temples, but the Sepoys were allowed to worship their regimental colours, and display their Ramhita exploits on the different parade-grounds. Besides all this, there has been a great favouritism shown to men of high caste, and the native army was almost exclusively made up of men of this character; and that which has been so fostered, even to infatuation, has sprung up and resulted in untold misery and desolation. God has by the mutiny spoken in an unmistakeable manner to the Indian Government, and we trust that the lessons taught will not pass without being duly considered. We cannot believe that India is to be lost, but rather benefited greatly by the changes which are now to be inaugurated, and carried on to completion. It is only such a development as has been made, and made too in such a manner as to impress all classes, that could convince the governing powers in Leadenhall-street, London, of the folly and sinfulness of their former course and opinions. The Government must no longer mislead the people by false statements, wicked compliances, or the repressing of all truth whatever. All that tends to foster superstition and encourage false religions must be discontinued, and perfect liberty of conscience must be allowed to all classes, independent of all aid or sanction from the powers that be. Let the temples of Kalee and Juggernaut receive no more or less protection and encouragement than the churches of the Christians. What is requested is, that all classes, whatever be their religion, should enjoy equally the most perfect freedom of worship consistent with good morals, and every degree of proper toleration; and, with respect to Government schools, high or low, we must insist on no more exclusion of the word of God. This is a point of vital importance to the welfare of India and her rulers. We must have no more such graduates as Nana Sahib to go forth into the world to sow the seeds of rebellion, and imbue their hands in the blood of Christians, whom they have been taught to despise and hate in the nurseries of infidelity, supported and encouraged by Government.

"This may be regarded as strong language, but for its truth and propriety we must appeal to facts to sustain us, and on such occasions we think truth ought to be spoken boldly and honestly. The exclusion of God's word and the expurgation of the name of the Saviour from the books taught in these schools, is a stigma under which good men have withered and suffered.

"We know of one of the ablest and best men in the civil service, who, because of his refusal to have any connexion with these schools, was not only refused promotion granted to others, but was degraded by being kept in a position of less power and emolument. He was hung, after undergoing a mock trial at Bareilly, by the mutineers. This system must be changed. To allow a place to the Koran or Shasters, and not to the Bible, can be characterized only by the strongest language of disapprobation, and deserves the reprobation it so justly merits at the hands of all Christian men. The very statement that the most puerile productions might be read and studied, but not a word of God's revelation of mercy and love, is enough to condemn the system hitherto pursued by Government.

"We trust that this will be one of the good effects accomplished by the present rebellion; and if so, what a glorious result will be achieved for the future interests of the people of India!"

[The author of this Essay considers that the above condemnation of the system pursued in Government schools is too sweeping. He adds, as a corrective to the vehement language quoted above, the calm and temperate expression of opinion in Bishop Gell's *Primary Charge*, delivered in Madras, April 23, 1863. With that opinion the author most thoroughly agrees.

"As regards the great question of Government Education, and the use of the Bible in all our schools: I think we ought to acknowledge with thankfulness; first, that there are Christian masters at the head of some of the Government schools who care for the souls as well as the intellects of those whom they are appointed to teach; and secondly, that books are used in which distinctive Christian principles and facts are mentioned. We ought also to remember, how undesirable it would be, that the teaching of the Bible should be entrusted to a heathen master whose principles might encourage rather than check him in turning the solemn and holy teaching of God's word into ridicule, and poisoning, not elevating, his pupil's mind.

"But what seems to be a matter for regret in the position which Government has taken is this. Their leading principle has the appearance of being the protection of heathenism, not the encouragement of Christianity. *It excludes the Bible, with exceptions; instead of including it, with exceptions.* It says, you shall not have the Bible unless you want and ask for it; and then not in school-hours; instead of saying, you shall have the Bible, unless you refuse it.

"It is possible that at first the practical carrying out of

one of these principles might, owing to the want of agents for teaching the Bible, be very much the same as that of the other. But in the long run they will be very different. And I believe that one is in accordance with the mind of God. The Gospel word is, Come : we have good things for you, come and see. And the faithful Stewards of the Gospel throw open their heavenly treasures, that whosoever is willing may come and see.

"And the Government, whose chief glory is that it is a Christian Government, does best when it remembers that Christian truth is its foundation, Christian love its great principle of action, the establishment of the kingdom of Christ among all its subjects its ultimate and far highest object.

"It is very possible that thus far even if Government had announced itself twenty years ago to all India as Christian, and shown favour to the study of the Scriptures in all cases without enforcing it in any, there might nevertheless be even now very few schools in which the Bible was so studied. But the number must have been somewhat greater than it is; and humanly speaking, it would have gone on increasing, and the open acknowledgment of the name of Christ would have been also openly acknowledged and blessed by Him who is 'King of kings and Lord of lords,' before whom ere long 'all kings shall fall down, and all nations do Him service,' yea, 'all dominions shall serve and obey Him,' and 'He shall reign for ever and ever.'

"It is not unreasonable to expect that as during the last fifty years the governing powers of India have gradually recognized great Christian principles which once they opposed to such an extent as even to forbid the presence of a Christian missionary, so they will move onwards until all Christian principles are recognized, and the very best that can be done for this land and its great population by sanctified human Government shall be done."]

The extract from Kaye is as follows: "As to what, rightly considered, that experience has taught us, there may be differences of opinion, but it is easy to understand the policy of our predecessors, without conceiving that it necessarily indicates any love for the unclean thing; or that the many evils, which from time to time necessarily grew out of this State patronage, are proofs of the unchristian character either of the Government or its executive officers. But when account was taken of these evils, doubtless they were very serious. Special attention has been directed to the idolatry of Juggernauth, which, by reason of its gigantic proportions and its excessive monstrosity, has always stood forth, in the sight of European nations, as the great representative of the idolatries of the Indies. But Government connexion with idolatry extended itself over the whole country, and as new provinces passed under British rule, new examples of this unholy alliance arose to swell the great sum-total of our practical heathenism. Such things were then regarded as the necessities of our position. Leaping suddenly into the throne of a heathen prince—as at Poonah, or other places easily to be named—we took up, as we had done elsewhere before, the said prince's liabilities, without regard to the nature of the contract; and to the discharge of them we doubtless entered into details of administration very repugnant to the feelings of Christian men. Not merely did the State afford protection to idolatry by securing to it the endowments it had enjoyed under the native rulers of the country, but it entered, in a variety of ways, into the internal management of the pagodas and the regulation of their ceremonies, and actively participated in what it would have been sufficient to passively tolerate. It was done with good intentions I do not doubt; rather, perhaps, it should be said in furtherance of a good principle. Without some such intervention and supervision of the State, the property was in a fair way to be misappropriated by the priests; and what the Government really intended to do was simply to protect Molech against the felonies of his own servants, and see that his business was conducted in a proper methodical way. 'If we are to do it at all,' it was said in those days, 'we may as well do it handsomely. A corrupt heathen church is no worse than a well-ordered one. What is Christianity to gain by ecclesiastical abuses and hierarchical frauds in the bosom of Hindooism?' So thought those who thought anything about the matter. But many did not think at all. They went about this work as about any other work. They collected the idol tribute; saw that it was devoted to its proper uses; that the servants of the temple were duly paid; its ceremonies properly performed, and the necessary repairs executed in a proper workmanlike way. Now this was something beyond neutrality; something more than mere toleration. Such as it was, too, it went on in many parts of the country for years. Nor was it merely in the administration of the revenues of idolatry and the superintendence of its establishments that our tender regard for the heathenism of the people evinced itself. We made much open display of our reverence for their institutions by attendance at their festivals; turning out our troops to give additional effect to the show, firing salutes in honour of their highdays and holidays, and sanctioning, nay, promoting, the prayers and invocations of the Brahmans to propitiate the deity for a good harvest or a good trade.

"The mismanagement of the native officials themselves, the injustice, perhaps, which was being done to the many by the few, only roused the sympathies of the European functionary, who, looking at the case only as between man and man, did, from a pure love of justice, what he might have shrunk from doing had he regarded the issue as one between Christianity and idolatry. Knowing that he himself had no other thought than that of doing justice to his neighbour, irrespectively of all conflicting creeds, it did not occur to him that his actions might be misjudged, and that, however remote may have been his intentions from all thought of encouraging Hindooism, it was impossible to dissever the knowledge of his acts from such associations in the minds of the people. It was not the thing itself, so much as the interpretation put upon it, that was injurious to Christianity; for it was impossible to disabuse the native mind of the belief that the English Government, which exhibited so tender a regard for the welfare of the idolatrous institutions of the country, was really anxious to perpetuate them."

Note P. Page 92.

The Rev. ROBERT C. KING, of the Colonial Church and School Society, Liverpool, remarked "that one great opportunity for the evangelization of the heathen rested with their own people scattered amongst them. It had been a matter of regret to every one connected with direct missionary work, that there was so much practical negligence found among our own people who permeated the mass of heathen. Missionaries bore testimony that there was a far greater difficulty in 'making way' in the large towns than in the country districts. He held in his hand a communication from a Secretary of the Church Missionary Society stating that the proportion of converts in the rural populations was far larger than in the towns; and the reason was obvious; for in towns there was a larger European element, and consequent immorality; so that when the missionaries pointed to the theory of Christianity, the heathen pointed to the practice of Christians; for the natives *would* look to see what kind of people Christianity makes, and what kind of a thing it was in its working out. When, therefore, they talked of getting candidates of the right stamp for the missionary work, they should not ignore the fact of their own people going up and down amongst the heathen, as they might; and being a great element for good by their example and conduct. They were watched far more than they imagined. He was quite sure the Conference would agree that if their own people, moving amongst the heathen, were what they professed to be, it would work directly and to a great extent in furtherance of their missionary labours. He thought this matter was worthy of their most serious attention."

The following passage is from a very interesting article by the late Bishop of Calcutta on the Tinnevelly Missions:

"One advantage, indeed, they have enjoyed which we are loath to mention, but which we suspect has told far more in favour of their cause than any assumption of the character of fakirs would have done. There is scarcely any part of India which is more removed from contact with Europeans than Tinnevelly. Dr Caldwell says that in many of its secluded districts the peasants have never seen the face of an English layman. Now it is quite true that no healthier influence can be exercised over a Hindu village than that of a brave, manly, and energetic English magistrate or settler, especially if his home is graced and purified by the presence of a good wife, not uninterested in the people around her. We thankfully acknowledge that such examples of the

Christian life are becoming more and more frequent, but still we must confess with shame that too often the conduct of the English in India has been quite the reverse of this, and that their lives have often furnished the most formidable arguments against the religion which they profess. We are painfully convinced that the grievous inconsistency of European nominal Christians, and not any want of self-sacrifice in the missionaries, has been hitherto one principal reason why the progress of Christianity in India has been so slow and disappointing. Such a hindrance however has but rarely opposed the truth in Tinnevelly : the people have seen the Christian life exhibited to them only in its very best and purest form, and it is not wonderful that they have been attracted by it."

Dr Lockhart, the first medical missionary sent to China, by the London Missionary Society, in the course of an address made at the Liverpool Conference in 1860, made the following remarks :

"Before I close," he said, " I would allude for a moment to one thing which has been found a great obstacle to the success of missions in all Eastern and heathen countries; and in a sea-port like this I would speak of it with all the power and emphasis that I can employ. I refer to the debauchery, licentiousness, and wickedness of our sailors, who go forth and sow the seeds of wickedness and sin in all heathen lands, and in none more than in China. It makes the heart of the missionary sad indeed to see his work day by day undone by the wickedness and debauchery of these sailors. It is the same in the ports of India, in the South Seas, in Africa, and in the West Indies. When the Chinese see, for instance, our sailors on leave ashore on the Sabbath-day getting drunk, going into the various villages, and by their violence and wickedness setting the minds of the people against them, they naturally say to us, 'You teachers come and preach the gospel of Jesus Christ; do you call these men Christians? Is it to make us like these that you preach to us the Gospel of Christ?' And what can we say in reply? Here are men from Christian England exhibiting not the fruits of holiness, but of wickedness and sin. I call your attention to this great obstacle to the success of missions, because much can be done by getting the fact thoroughly known in England, that this *more than anything else I know of*, interferes with our success."

[The author of this Essay, when in India, heard of the following occurrence:

A missionary and a catechist were at Trichinopoly preaching to the heathen. Whilst some natives were listening, a drunken English soldier came up, pushing his way amongst them, and talking in a loud and violent manner. Seeing the condition of the man the heathen turned it to account on their side of the discussion, and called out, jeeringly, "Make way, make way! here is one of the Guru's disciples." And what could the "Guru" (*i.e.* the missionary, literally priest,) reply so as to efface the unfavourable impression caused?]

Note Q. P. 93.

"It will be hard, we think, to find compensation, not only to Australia, but to New Zealand, and to the innumerable islands of the South Seas, for the murders, the misery, the contamination which we have brought upon them. Our runaway convicts are the pests of savage as well as of civilized society; so are our runaway sailors; and the crews of our whaling vessels, and of the traders from New South Wales, too frequently act in the most reckless and immoral manner when at a distance from the restraints of justice: in proof of this we need only refer to the evidence of the missionaries.

"It is stated that there have been not less than 150 or 250 runaways at once on the island of New Zealand, counteracting all that was done for the moral improvement of the people, and teaching them every vice.

"'I beg leave to add,' remarks Mr Ellis, 'the desirableness of preventing, by every practicable means, the introduction of ardent spirits among the inhabitants of the countries we may visit or colonize. There is nothing more injurious to the South Sea islanders than seamen who have absconded from ships, setting up huts for the retail of ardent spirits, called grog-shops, which are the resort of the indolent and vicious of the crews of the vessels, and in which, under the influence of intoxication, scenes of immorality, and even murder, have been exhibited, almost beyond what the natives witnessed among themselves while they were heathen. The demoralization and impediments to the civilization and prosperity of the people that have resulted from the activity of foreign traders in ardent spirits, have been painful in the extreme. In one year it is estimated that the sum of 12,000 dollars was expended, in Taheité alone, chiefly by the natives, for ardent spirits.'

"The lawless conduct of the crews of vessels must necessarily have an injurious effect on our trade, and on that ground alone demands investigation. In the month of April, 1834, Mr Busby states there were twenty-nine vessels at one time in the Bay of Islands; and that seldom a day passed without some complaint being made to him of the most outrageous conduct on the part of their crews, which he had not the means of repressing, since these reckless seamen totally disregarded the usages of their own country, and the unsupported authority of the British resident.

"The Rev. J. Williams, missionary in the Society Islands, states, 'that it is the common sailors, and the lowest order of them, the very vilest of the whole, who will leave their ship and go to live amongst the savages, and take with them all their low habits and all their vices.' The captains of merchant vessels are apt to connive at the absconding of such worthless sailors, and the atrocities perpetrated by them are excessive; they do incalculable mischief by circulating reports injurious to the interests of trade. On an island between the Navigator's and the Friendly group, he heard there were on one occasion a hundred sailors who had run away from shipping. Mr Williams gives an account of a gang of convicts who stole a small vessel from New South Wales, and came to Raiatia, one of the Sandwich Islands, where he resided, representing themselves as shipwrecked mariners. Mr Williams suspected them, and told them he should inform the governor, Sir T. Brisbane, of their arrival, on which they went away to an island twenty miles off, and were received with every kindness in the house of the chief. They took an opportunity of stealing a boat belonging to the missionary of the station, and made off again. The natives immediately pursued, and desired them to return their missionary's boat. Instead of replying, they discharged a blunderbuss that was loaded with cooper's rivets, which blew the head of one man to pieces; they then killed two more, and a fourth received the contents of a blunderbuss in his hand, fell from exhaustion amongst his mutilated companions, and was left as dead. This man, and a boy who had saved himself by diving, returned to their island. 'The natives were very respectable persons; and had it not been that we were established in the estimation of the people, our lives would have been sacrificed. The convicts then went in the boat down to the Navigator's Islands, and there entered with savage ferocity into the wars of the savages. One of these men was the most savage monster that ever I heard of: he boasted of having killed 300 natives with his own hands.'

"And in June 1833, Mr Thomas, Wesleyan missionary at the Friendly Islands, still speaks of the mischief done by ill-disposed captains of whalers, who, he says, 'send the refuse of their crews on shore to annoy us;' and proceeds to state, 'the conduct of many of these masters of South-Sea whalers is most abominable; they think no more of the life of an heathen than of a dog. And their cruel and wanton behaviour at the different islands in those seas has a powerful tendency to lead the natives to hate the sight of a white man.' Mr Williams mentions one of these captains, who with his people had shot twenty natives, at one of the islands, for no offence; and 'another master of a whaler, from Sidney, made his boast, last Christmas, at Tonga, that he had killed about twenty black fellows,—for so he called the natives of the Samoa, or Navigator's Islands—for some very trifling offence; and not satisfied with that, he designed to disguise his vessel, and pay them another visit, and get about a hundred more of them.' 'Our hearts,' continues Mr Thomas, 'almost bleed for the poor Samoa people; they are a very mild, inoffensive race, very easy of access; and as they are near to us, we have a great hope of their embracing the truth, viz. that the whole group will do so; for you will learn from Mr Williams' letter, that a part of them have already turned to God. But the conduct of our English savages has a tone of barbarity and cruelty in it which was never heard of or practised by them.'

"But these are not all the exploits of these white savages. Those who have seen in shop-windows in London, dried heads of New Zealanders, may here learn how they come there, and to whom the phrenologists and *curiosi* are indebted.

"Till lately the tattooed heads of New Zealanders were sold at Sidney as objects of curiosity; and Mr Yate says he has known people give property to a chief for the purpose of getting them to kill their slaves, that they might have some heads to take to New South Wales.

"This degrading traffic was prohibited by General Darling, the governor, upon the following occasion: In a representation made to Governor Darling, the Rev. Mr Marsden states, that the captain of an English vessel being, as he conceived, insulted by some native women, set one tribe upon another to avenge his quarrel, and supplied them with arms and ammunition to fight.

"In the prosecution of the war thus excited, a party of forty-one Bay of Islanders made an expedition against some tribes of the South. Forty of the former were cut off; and a few weeks after the slaughter, a Captain Jack went and purchased thirteen chiefs' heads, and, bringing them back to the Bay of Islands, emptied them out of a sack in presence of their relations. The New Zealanders were, very properly, so much enraged that they told this captain they should take possession of the ship, and put the laws of their country into execution. When he found that they were in earnest, he cut his cable and left the harbour, and afterwards had a narrow escape from them at Taurunga. He afterwards reached Sidney, and it came to the knowledge of the governor, that he brought there ten of these heads for sale, on which discovery the practice was declared unlawful. Mr Yate mentions an instance of a captain going 300 miles from the Bay of Islands to East Cape, enticing twenty-five young men, sons of chiefs, on board his vessel, and delivering them to the Bay of Islanders, with whom they were at war, merely to gain the favour of the latter, and to obtain supplies for his vessel. The youths were afterwards redeemed from slavery by the missionaries, and restored to their friends. Mr Yate once took from the hand of a New Zealand chief a packet of corrosive sublimate, which a captain had given to the savage in order to enable him to poison his enemies."

www.ingramcontent.com/pod-product-compliance
Lightning Source LLC
Chambersburg PA
CBHW030257170426
43202CB00009B/781